Prince Friedrich of Homburg

Prince Friedrich

of

Homburg

A drama by Heinrich von Kleist

TRANSLATED WITH A CRITICAL INTRODUCTION
BY DIANA STONE PETERS AND FREDERICK G. PETERS

A NEW DIRECTIONS BOOK

TO OUR PARENTS

Manufactured in the United States of America
First published clothbound and as New Directions Paperbook 462 in 1978
Published simultaneously in Canada by McClelland & Stewart, Ltd.

Library of Congress Cataloging in Publication Data
Kleist, Heinrich von, 1777-1811.
    Prince Friedrich of Homburg.
    (A New Directions Book)
    I. Peters, Diana Stone   II. Peters, Frederick G.
III. Title.
PT2378.P73P4   832'.6   78-6670
ISBN 0-8112-0709-9
ISBN 0-8112-0694-7 pbk.

New Directions Books are published for James Laughlin
by New Directions Publishing Corporation,
333 Sixth Avenue, New York 10014

Introduction

I

Heinrich von Kleist, who committed suicide at the age of thirty-four shortly after completing one of the finest dramas in the German language, was born in Frankfurt on the Oder on October 18, 1777. Although his short existence was marked by a series of never-ending failures and an ever-present sense of personal disgrace and shame, Kleist's life began in promising circumstances with his birth into an aristocratic Prussian family. As the descendant of a long and distinguished line of army officers, however, he was unfortunately predestined for a military career: Kleist entered a Potsdam regiment at the age of fifteen and took part in a campaign in the Rhineland against the French Revolutionary armies. But after seven years of service—each of which he thoroughly loathed—he asked for his release in order to study mathematics and philosophy at his hometown university. Kleist's abilities and temperament made military life as inappropriate for him as it was for the American writer Edgar Allen Poe, who was dismissed from the United States Military Academy at West Point after one year. Henceforth, Kleist embarked on a ceaseless quest to discover a profession or even a way of life suited to his often bizarre and always uncompromising temperament.

A shy, sullen, and solitary person, plagued by a speech defect as well as by hypochondria, Kleist's conduct in society was marked by spasmodic fits of embarrassment and blushing. His personality seemed to vacillate in a repelling fashion between extremes: thus, a delicate conscience and an almost pathological sensitivity to the remarks of others did not prevent him from occasionally behaving in a tactless and cruel fashion. Possessed of a profound sense of inferiority, Kleist also reveled in the euphoric conviction that he was destined to displace Goethe as Germany's greatest writer. His feelings of unworthiness and deep depression often found outlet in outbursts of rage against a world that ignored his genius. Despite a long period of engagement, in which he pedantically attempted to instruct his fiancée in how to become a suitable wife for him, Kleist never felt able to commit himself to marriage and so remained a bachelor throughout his life. Not surprisingly, the artistic fulfillment and personal happiness which he so desperately sought continued to elude him. Near the end of his life, he wrote: "The truth is that there was no help for me on earth."

In addition to the difficulties that Kleist's temperament may have caused him, there is little doubt but that the external world also colluded to destroy him. The shocks that he sustained from outside, particularly during the last year of his life (1810–11), were too great and too many for him to overcome, given his increasing exhaustion, pessimism, and despair. Berlin's first daily newspaper, *Die Berliner Abendblätter*, which Kleist had founded, collapsed at this time, due in part to the pressure of government censorship. (His literary periodical, *Phöbus,* had failed shortly before, in 1809.) His patroness, Queen Louise, died, and a small pension that he had been receiving from her came to a sudden halt. The first performance of *Prince Friedrich of Homburg* was unexpectedly canceled at the last moment, and Kleist was also experiencing difficulties with the publication of his other dramas. At the age of thirty-four, then, he found himself unemployed and penniless, ostracized by his family, and unappreciated by the public. He wondered sadly: "Really, it's strange how everything I undertake at present seems bound to come to nothing; how whenever I decide to take a firm step the ground simply vanishes from under my feet."

If anything or anyone could have rescued Kleist from his

suicidal depression, it would have been an encouraging word from Goethe, to whom Kleist had sent his play *Penthesilea* "on the knees of [his] heart." But Goethe continued to be not merely unsympathetic; he was positively repulsed by the violence of emotion in Kleist's works and by their apparent lack of moral restraint and aesthetic discipline. Now securely wrapped in the mantle of his Olympian serenity, Goethe believed that art should glorify the noblest possibilities inherent in man's nature, whereas Kleist's works, embodying a very unedifying and morbid vision of man, seemed to him only to present a series of pathological case studies. Goethe once admitted: "With the best will in the world toward this poet [Kleist], I have always been moved to horror and disgust by something in his works, as though here were a body well planned by nature, tainted with an incurable disease."

Assessing the result of his years of herculean struggle, Kleist had to admit that failure had followed all of his most varied attempts to secure a hold upon life: in the practical world of journalism, in his attempts to marry and found a home, and in his extravagant hope to dethrone Goethe. He could only believe that he was "a useless member of society, no longer worthy of any sympathy." At this lowest point in his life, Kleist met and formed a suicide pact with a married woman, Henriette Vogel, who was suffering from an incurable cancer. They died by the pistol on Lake Wannsee near Potsdam on November 21, 1811. His creative period, which encompassed barely ten years, had yielded eight plays and eight short stories, all of which he believed would be forgotten along with himself. But history has proved Kleist's extreme pessimism to have been wrong. A more correct estimate of the fate of his work and reputation appears as the epitaph upon his tombstone:

> He lived and sang and suffered
> in dreary, difficult times.
> Here he sought death
> and found undying fame.

II

A critical approach to the central issues in *Prince Friedrich of Homburg* requires a brief introductory discussion of the principal trauma in Kleist's emotional and intellectual life: his reading and misunderstanding of Kant's philosophy in 1801. Before this experience, Kleist had professed to extremely optimistic views concerning man's ability to perfect himself and thus find happiness on earth. Since God's existence guaranteed for Kleist a rational world order, he believed that it was within man's power to approach truth through the exercise of human reason. When Kleist decided in 1799 to study at the university, he was not primarily motivated by the need to satisfy a general intellectual curiosity. Rather, his systematic acquisition of knowledge was directed toward the formation of a rational life-plan that would gradually allow him to bring his daily life into harmony with the absolute. But his so-called Kant crisis convinced him that the quest for truth through an accumulation of knowledge was a futile exercise. He interpreted Kant's philosophy as proving that the mind of man can never grasp and know ultimate truth but is forever condemned to perceiving at most the mere appearance of things: human reason can thus accumulate only illusion and falsehood. Kleist was plunged into the darkest despair: "My one supreme goal has vanished, and I am bereft." The reading of a book had apparently robbed his life of all meaning and purpose.

Kleist's philosophical disenchantment only masked with an abstract terminology a more primitive and personal crisis. His discovery of Kant coincided with a period in his life when he was beginning to perceive that his volcanic emotions could no longer be held in check by a belief in the supreme power of reason to subdue and contain the feelings. Kant's philosophy, by apparently dethroning the power of reason to perceive the truth, provided Kleist with an objective explanation for the fact that his life was now no less in turmoil than before he had begun his studies of mathematics and logic. Kleist suddenly felt himself set dangerously adrift upon a sea of chaotic emotions. His urgent need to regain inner stability was not to be accomplished (for instance) by anchoring his life to that of another human being. Rather, he eventually chose to affirm the relationship of the individual to the state, in which the individual voluntarily accepts the state as the embodiment of the sole existing absolute in a secular world without transcendence. The exploration of this relationship became a central theme in Kleist's last works: the story "Michael Kohlhaas" (1809) and his last two dramas, *The Battle of Arminius* (1808) and *Prince Friedrich of Homburg* (1811). Indeed, Kleist admitted that he intended *Prince Friedrich of Homburg* to be "a patriotic drama." Here, an egoistic individual learns to subordinate his infantile needs and fantasies to the collective good as defined by the state. It may be noted that some modern literary critics actually accuse Kleist of having glorified the mystique of Prussian nationalism to such a degree that they regard *Prince Friedrich of Homburg* as nothing less than a protofascist work.

Brecht's life and work provide a striking and illuminating parallel, for he, too, possessed a highly emotional and sensitive personality that often seemed at the mercy of compulsions beyond his conscious control. About 1930, however, he underwent an amazing dialectical reversal: he provided himself with an anchor in the objective world by becoming a fervent communist. Brecht affirmed the discipline of the party, which required the individual to sacrifice the needs of his own merely personal emotional life to the requirements of the common good as enumerated by the doctrines of the communist state. Thus, both Kleist and Brecht, feeling themselves threatened by the dangers of emotional isolation within their own pure subjectivity, as well as by the terrors of philosophical weightlessness in a world without God, affirmed the order and structure of external political authority. A twofold benefit accrued from such a decision: the tumultuous inner life could be disciplined as its importance was devalued, while at the same time the individual's existence was provided with a higher purpose as a social being through voluntary participation in the realization of the state's ever-growing power.

How, then, can the fact be explained that the government (respectively, Prussian and communist) took a most ambivalent, if not decidedly negative attitude toward those dramas of Kleist and Brecht in which they specifically intended to glorify the state? *Prince Friedrich of Homburg* was prevented from being performed in Berlin until 1828 because the Prussian King's sister-in-law, to whom Kleist had dedicated the work, objected that her noble ancestor, the Prince of Homburg, had been slandered in the play. The play had been performed in Vienna in 1821 but was closed by the police after five performances. The Archduke felt that the drama would have a demoralizing effect upon his army officers. It is well known that the communist party has always regarded Brecht's dramas with the greatest ambivalence and even suspicion. His works have rarely been allowed in the theaters of the Soviet Union but have instead been relegated to Brecht's theater in East Berlin, where they form part of the communists' artistic showcase to the West. In this sense, the Prussian and communist states revealed a greater understanding of these dramatic achievements than did the dramatists themselves. In treating the theme of the individual's relationship to the state, neither Kleist nor Brecht was able to suppress the psychological complexities and moral ambiguities inherent in such a relationship in order to deliver a simple propagandistic message. Because of their own ambivalence toward the inner life, they created more than they knew.

III

Prince Friedrich of Homburg is one of the most stageworthy plays ever written. In spite of the presence throughout of intense emotional conflict, often causing the characters to swing from ecstatic exultation to blackest depression and from reflective calm to total hysteria, Kleist nevertheless managed to produce a drama that is balanced and perfectly constructed, a work at once intellectually subtle and yet marked by constant action. Unlike some of his earlier plays, this last drama is never sententious, wordy, or static. Perhaps particularly striking in the work of a German writer is the perfect unity in this drama between the exploration of highly abstract problems and their presentation in very concrete and personal situations. In *Prince Friedrich of Homburg*, Kleist treats at one and the same time a rather abstract theoretical problem (the individual's relationship to the state), the most traumatic of human events (a man's anticipation of his own death by execution), and the presence and effect of hidden wishes upon behavior (the unacknowledged desires of the unconscious). And yet, as the themes develop and merge, the spectator's imagination is gripped primarily by the actual events of the play, which carry him forward without respite from the very first dreamlike scene to the play's extraordinary conclusion.

Kleist's exposition of his protagonist's character in the first scene is a brilliant stroke of dramatic genius. By introducing the Prince in a somnambulistic trance, Kleist is able to expose directly to the audience his character's deepest desires freed from the inhibitions that the waking mind usually exercises when individuals converse. Fragments of speech and gesture form a kind of monologue from the unconscious in which the Prince reveals himself to be a man obsessed with military fame and personal glory. Upon waking and going into battle, he expects that his dream will become reality and that the outer world will inevitably support his heroic vision of himself. But reality in the form of the Elector rises up to challenge his dreams, presenting an argument which in its abstract formulation is quite incomprehensible to the emotionally immature young Prince.

The Elector demands obedience. The fact that the Prince has won an important battle is irrelevant, for more battles will have to be fought. Therefore, the Elector prizes only a victory gained according to principles of strategy and not one brought about by the momentary and capricious inspiration of a single individual. The Prince cannot take such an argument seriously.

He is quite unable at this point to see the Elector as a wise, prudent, and farsighted ruler, the embodiment of objective law, concerned only with furthering the general good of the state. This is not surprising: were the Prince to accept the Elector's condemnation of his behavior on the battlefield, his heroic deed would be transformed into irresponsible, undisciplined, and impulsive conduct directed solely toward the immediate gratification of personal desires. Literary critics of the play have generally allied themselves either with the Prince or the Elector. Those supporting the Prince justify the right of the passionate individual to reject a cold and lifeless ruler's insistence upon subordination and mindless obedience to rigid and inflexible law. But whether Kleist's critics have come to the defense of the Elector or of the Prince, their language and argumentation have tended to be too intellectualized and too abstract to capture the most fundamental reality of the play: the inability of man, the animal, to face the certainty of his own death.

At the center of the drama, functioning as the ultimate symbol of unadorned reality, is the dark grave that is being dug for the Prince. It is before this abyss—and not before the Elector's abstract arguments—that the Prince's world of romantic dreams collapses completely. All thoughts of love and glory vanish. The Prince is now prepared to give up everything that he had once valued in order to be allowed merely to live at the lowest level of existence conceivable to him, as a farmer upon his distant estates. The Prince thus subscribes to the sentiment of another great warrior, Achilles, who admitted to Odysseus when the latter visited him in the underworld: it is better to live upon the earth as the humblest of men in the humblest of occupations than to reign as king over all the dead. The Prince, of course, has faced death countless times on the battlefield but, as the German existentialist Martin Heidegger writes, only in the self-deceiving way that most people regard death: either as something that happens to other people or as something that will eventually befall oneself but at another and much later time. At the sight of his open grave, however, the Prince is touched and overwhelmed for the first time by the horrible reality of death as an event that will inexorably overtake him in the near future: the courageous and proud Prince suddenly becomes an hysterical coward. It was precisely this unedifying spectacle of the Prince's breakdown that caused Archduke Charles to ban the play from the Austrian stage. He may well have acted on the assumption that the fear of personal death dangerously subverts the strength of all social and political ties.

A call from outside in the form of the Elector's letter penetrates into the Prince's isolation, a prison within a prison which Homburg has created by immersing himself totally in thoughts of his impending death. The Elector effects the Prince's return to the world of social and moral ties by treating him as a man capable of evaluating his own behavior in terms of the collective needs of the state, needs which the Elector believes must be superior even to the individual's instinctual need for self-preservation. When the Prince is given the freedom to choose, to control his own destiny, he admits to his astonished officers: "I want to die a freely chosen death." By voluntarily choosing to die, he transforms death from a mere brutal force that mechanically destroys into a glorious event that corrects and crowns his personal existence. No longer an irresponsible and self-centered youth, the Prince believes he will be ennobled through the sacrificial surrender of his life to the collective ideal of the state as embodied and articulated by the Elector.

Having affirmed the law of the state in his innermost heart, the Prince no longer perceives the law as brutally pressing upon him from outside. Paradoxically, now that the Prince recognizes as valid the rule of law that requires his execution, the Elector believes him to be worthy of pardon. Moreover, since the Prince has acted in the very manner anticipated by the Elector, the Elector is able to justify to himself and his officers his role as omniscient, godlike pedagogue. Glorification of the Elector as a Wise Old Man underlies most of the critical interpretations of *Prince Friedrich of Homburg*. This approach, however, places too much emphasis on an alleged process of education and the Elector's role in it. The central theme of the play is not a conflict between the needs of the individual and those of the state, but the problem of what the individual must do and must believe in order to be able to face certain death.

Since man is psychologically incapable of dying for nothing, the problem facing the Prince becomes one of finding a way to affirm his death. For, if it is a noble pursuit to give one's life meaning, it is an absolute necessity to give meaning to one's impending death. The key to such a psychological *tour de force* is guilt. It is the affirmation of personal guilt before an absolute —be it God, the father, or the state—that makes it possible for the individual to walk rather than be dragged to the place of execution. By means of this psychological process, death is not only transformed into a just punishment imposed from outside, it also gives the guilty individual the welcome opportunity to atone and cleanse himself. In *Prince Friedrich of Homburg,* the crucial step in this process of "personalizing" death occurs when the Prince reverses his earlier protestations of innocence and outrage and admits: "Guilt, grave guilt lies heavily upon me."

As a means of clarifying this psychological process, three other works by major writers may be cited which deal with precisely the same theme. Friedrich Schiller's imagination was so gripped by this problem that he violated historical fact in his play *Mary Stuart* (1800) in order to be able to present the protagonist's search for a meaningful death. Mary was executed in 1587 because of her certain involvement in a plot to assassinate Elizabeth, the Queen of England. In Schiller's drama, however, Mary is totally innocent of this particular crime, for which she must now ascend the scaffold. On the other hand, she did conspire to murder her second husband, Darnley, in 1567, a crime which has gone unpunished. Therefore, rather than suffering death as a purely external and thus meaningless event, Mary transforms Elizabeth, her executioner, into that unwitting force which permits her to atone before God for her earlier deed. Mary declares: "By this undeserved death [on the scaffold], God allows me to atone for an earlier bloody crime." With this thought in mind, Mary is able to walk with dignity and serenity to the scaffold.

In the twentieth century, Franz Kafka's short story "The Judgment" (1912) describes how the protagonist, Georg Bendemann, is condemned to death by his own father for various transgressions. Because he recognizes his guilt, the protagonist is able to carry out the verdict himself and dies happy and at peace with the world. Finally, Brecht's didactic play, *The Measures Taken,* which bears particularly close affinities to Kleist's drama, treats the fate of a young communist who admits that his personal feelings caused him to disobey the strict orders of the party, thus undermining its struggles with the enemy. He recognizes his guilt and voluntarily accepts execution for the good of the party. Thus, Prince Friedrich, Mary Stuart, Georg Bendemann, and the young comrade all manage to face their certain deaths by affirming their executioners. On the very threshold of death, each feels nothing but forgiveness and love in his heart for the human instrument of his destruction. By a process of voluntarily accepting guilt and punishment, these characters believe that their lives, previously marked by mere personal desire and petty whim, have been transformed and crowned by a higher meaning. Self-negation is the price of providing one's existence with transpersonal value, a value that can only be bestowed from outside by an absolute. Although the personal cost is the highest conceivable, the individual, by negating the self, liberates himself from the terrors inherent in thoughts of physical extinction.

The Prince's heroic transformation into a model citizen and soldier in the final scenes becomes readily comprehensible only from the perspective of his traumatic fear of death. He is no more mature at the end of the play than he was at the beginning, and he has not undergone a profound psychological development. Rather, the vision of his grave has precipitated a dialectical reversal of his persona. Beneath his new-found self-denying attitude of humility toward the state is now a greater egoism than ever before. His ego has expanded, as it were, to include within its personal self the glory and immortality of the whole state. He declares to his comrades that victory on the battlefield is paltry in comparison to victory over one's worst inner enemies, defiance and arrogance. But the Prince expects a reward for such personal victory, namely the freedom to die an exemplary death both in order to atone to the state and to affirm its eternal rules of law before others. He is veritably overcome by thoughts of this higher, more sublime act of heroism, an act which will be quite as public as was his victory over the Swedish enemy. Thus, the desire for fame and distinction continues as before to be the hallmark of his character. His yearning to die for the good of the state is as irrational as were his earlier dreams of personal glory in the moonlit castle garden. Therefore, the dazzling romantic conclusion of the drama is totally appropriate. Rather than being merely a superfluous conclusion tacked on to the end of the play for reasons of symmetry or because Kleist wished to conclude the work in a fashion both visually striking and highly dramatic, its parallels to the first scene emphasize that the dream of the state has but replaced a dream of the self; the Prince remains a dreamer. The mind of man cannot face the fact of death for more than a very short period of time. Thus, the existence of death in a world without the metaphysical absolute of God has generated a new illusion, the secular absolute of the state.

The modern spectator, having witnessed in recent history the systematic moral corruption of willing individuals living under totalitarian regimes, cannot help but experience the Prince's ecstatic affirmation of the Elector and the state with ambivalence. Of course, such ambivalence would be completely unjustified if the Elector were an unflawed, quasi-divine figure of justice and truth. But the Elector, whose motives for judgment should transcend the human-all-too-human factors which taint the behavior of lesser men, acts in several irrational ways which are not explicable in terms of the duties of his office and which are potentially more disruptive to the state's well-being than was the Prince's impulsive charge into battle. Three in-

stances may be cited which reveal the presence in the Elector
of deep-seated feelings of competition and jealousy arising from
his fear that he will eventually be overshadowed and displaced
by the Prince, whom he has raised from boyhood as his son.

The presence of the father-son configuration, from which the
unconscious mutual rivalry derives, is immediately revealed by
the Prince himself, who, in his dream, addresses the Elector
and the Electress as father and mother, which in reality they
are not. The Elector-father, driven at once by curiosity and by
fear of what he may yet discover, tempts the Prince to further
revelations by way of a test: he offers him his chain of office,
a wreath symbolizing heroic victory, and his niece and ward,
Princess Natalia, as well. When the Prince accepts everything
so naturally, the Elector, perhaps shocked at seeing his own
secret fear confirmed, becomes quite embarrassed at having
eavesdropped upon the Prince's innermost feelings.

As a direct consequence of this revelation, the Elector assigns
the ambitious and exuberant Prince a passive role in a decisive
battle, while he himself, the mature leader and battle's strate-
gist, takes the most active and heroic role in the forefront of
the assault. Moreover, as if to secure his position as the center
of interest, he has the vanity to ride a gleaming white horse
into the fray. Before the battle is over, however, the Prince and
the Elector exchange roles again, as if to confirm that the origi-
nal assignments were unnatural.

The Elector's error is twofold and has the gravest consequences both for the state and for several individuals. First, he
jeopardizes his own life needlessly, thereby also jeopardizing
the future of Prussia, which, at this point in its history, requires
stable and mature leadership. The Elector's vanity also costs
the life of his faithful groom, Froben, who finally persuades
his master to let him ride the white horse, whereupon he is immediately struck down by enemy bullets intended for the Elector. Second, the Elector has good cause to know that the Prince
is unable to await orders passively; the impetuous young Homburg has already cost the Elector two previous victories because

of his impulsive conduct. Moreover, the Elector tells the Prince during the dream scene that the fame, the glory, and the love he seeks are not to be won in dreams but are only earned upon the battlefield. The Elector therefore appears to have put the Prince in a position where he will be forced into disobeying his orders. However, by breaking the law in this manner, the Prince runs headlong not into the Elector himself but into his impersonal military court. In other words, if the Elector cannot eclipse the Prince by heroism in battle, he is still able to don the mask of head of state and allow the law to take its course, thereby ridding himself of the Prince without having to recognize the personal nature of the conflict. But this maneuver in turn has the effect of jeopardizing the state once again, for the Prince's imprisonment and the court-martial's harsh sentence threaten to bring the army to the point of insurrection, thereby undermining that very rule of law which the Elector is supposedly affirming by remaining aloof and refusing to pardon the Prince as he is empowered to do.

Finally, since the Elector acts not from stupidity but from unconscious motives, it becomes apparent why he feels he must allow the law to punish the Prince so severely for his small transgression while he is able to ignore and even condone what may be viewed as the far more treasonable acts of Kottwitz and Natalia, both of whom seem to be part of a conspiracy to free the Prince by force. It should be added in defense of the Elector's perception of the danger facing him, if not of the hypocritical manner in which he chooses to deal with it, that the threat from the Prince is a real one. Upon the apparent death of the Elector in battle, the Prince immediately (if naïvely) advances into the center of the Elector's family and his state: he declares that henceforth he will assume the protection of the Elector's throne as well as of Natalia, whom he now expects to marry forthwith. News of the Prince's precipitate assumption of the Elector's position was doubtless innocently conveyed to him by the Electress. The Elector's response is equally precipitate: without further inquiry as to the Prince's fault, he simply assumes the Prince took part in battle, disobeyed his orders, and must be sentenced to death.

A comparison with Kafka's short story "The Judgment" provides a most economical way of illuminating a pivotal occurrence in the denouement of the father-son rivalry in Kleist's drama. In Kafka's work, the father accuses the son, Georg, of subtly and hypocritically attempting to usurp his position in the world. But the most blatant single act of aggression against the father, which now causes him to condemn Georg to death, is his son's plan to marry; for by establishing his own family Georg will be forcing his father into the periphery of active life. In Kleist's play, Count Hohenzollern has a similar perception: totally ignoring the question of the Prince's military insubordination, Hohenzollern suggests, while visiting the Prince in prison, that the real reason for the Elector's disfavor arises from the Prince's rashly announced plan to marry Natalia without ever having obtained prior permission. That the Prince so readily accepts this explanation points to the presence of unconscious guilt feelings at having transgressed the Elector's right to control Natalia's destiny. Hence, the Prince immediately gives her up. And Natalia, as if having a presentiment of the rivalry between the Elector and the Prince, not only also renounces the Prince but, in her pleading for mercy before the Elector, stresses that the Prince has been reduced to a state of total capitulation: he is no longer the romantic hero on horseback, no longer the suitor for her hand. The Elector may now pardon him, may even reward him generously with Natalia's hand, because he is no longer a rival.

Has the Elector been affected by the events that he has precipitated? He must recognize that he himself has acted both too impulsively and too rigidly. Those closest to him—Hohenzollern, Natalia, and Kottwitz—have not spared him the most severe criticism. The Elector's miscalculation of the army's reaction to the Prince's death sentence has almost led to insurrection. He is, indeed, tottering on the edge of disaster when he is suddenly inspired to place the Prince's fate in his own hands by sending him the letter. Unknown to everyone but himself, the Elector's fate and that of the state, too, now lie in the hands of the Prince, who does, most fortunately, emerge to teach the rebellious soldiers the Elector's lessons of obedience to the law. The Elector alone knows how easily his improvised strategy could have failed.

Whereas the Prince reveals his every thought and feeling throughout the play to anyone who will listen and thus provides the actor with a brilliantly histrionic role, the Elector hides his reactions beneath the lofty impersonality of his office. Thus, his role is the more subtle and difficult one, for he must be played not as a figure of divine truth and not as a pompous moralizer but rather as a lonely and sometimes frightened man. Though the Prince undergoes a radical external change while remaining inwardly essentially the same, the Elector has the reverse experience.

The Elector's final situation in the play lends a certain tragic dignity to his life. The Prince in a rather childlike fashion has found a new anchor for his chaotic existence in his blind adoration of the Elector and the state. But where can the Elector find comfort and security, now that he has so profoundly experienced "the inherent weakness in the world's order" (*"die Gebrechlichkeit der Welt"*), not only as it menaces the happiness of the individual but also as it threatens the stability of the state?

Diana Stone Peters
Frederick G. Peters
Columbia University in the City of New York
November 1977

Prince Friedrich of Homburg

To Her Royal Highness
Princess Amalie Marie Anne,
née Princess of Hessen-Homburg,
wife of Prince Wilhelm of Prussia,
Brother of His Majesty the King.

The poet, plunged in the middle of the turbulent affairs of ordinary men, plucks the strings of his harp as he gazes up toward the heavens. The sounds he creates sometimes bring comfort and other times sorrow, but he cannot delight in any answer to his song. And yet he believes there's one within the crowded circle to whom he can dedicate his innermost feelings. She holds the prize in her hands which will fall to him, and if she crowns him, then he is crowned by all the world.

DRAMATIS PERSONAE

FRIEDRICH WILHELM, the Elector of Brandenburg

THE ELECTRESS, his wife

PRINCESS NATALIA OF ORANGE, his niece; commander-in-chief of a regiment of dragoons

FIELD MARSHAL DÖRFLING

PRINCE FRIEDRICH ARTHUR OF HOMBURG, general in charge of the cavalry

COLONEL KOTTWITZ, of the Princess of Orange's regiment

HENNINGS
COUNT TRUCHSS } infantry colonels

COUNT HOHENZOLLERN, attached to the Elector's suite

CAVALRY CAPTAIN VON DER GOLTZ

COUNT GEORGE VON SPARREN
STRANTZ } cavalry captains
SIEGFRIED VON MÖRNER

COUNT REUSS

A SERGEANT

Officers, corporals, cavalrymen; courtiers, ladies-in-waiting; pages, castle guards dressed as Hungarian foot soldiers; servants; people of every age and sex.

Act I

SCENE 1

Scene: Fehrbellin. A garden in the old French style. In the background a castle from which a ramp descends. It is night.

[*The Prince of Homburg, bareheaded and dressed in a shirt open in front, is seated under an oak tree—half asleep, half awake. He is weaving a wreath. The Elector, his wife, Princess Natalia, Count Hohenzollern, Cavalry Captain Goltz, and others steal secretly from the castle and look down upon him from the railing of the ramp. Pages with torches.*]

HOHENZOLLERN: There is our brave cousin, the Prince of Homburg, who, at the head of his troops, has been vigorously chasing the retreating Swedish army for the past three days. He's just now returned to headquarters here at Fehrbellin, completely out of breath. But didn't you give him quite specific orders not to remain here longer than the three hours necessary to procure supplies? Wasn't he then supposed to advance to the Hackelberg and wait there for our attack against the Swedish General Wrangel, who has been trying to entrench himself along the Rhyn?

ELECTOR: That's correct.

HOHENZOLLERN: Well, now, the leaders of all the squadrons, in accordance with this plan, were instructed to prepare to leave the city at the stroke of ten, but the Prince—he throws himself upon a pile of straw like a panting hunting dog and wants to rest his weary bones for a while before the coming battle starts at daybreak.

ELECTOR: So I've heard—and?

HOHENZOLLERN: The hour has struck, the whole cavalry is mounted, the horses are pawing at the ground before the city gates—and who's still missing? The Prince of Homburg, their leader! Our hero is sought with torches, lights, and lanterns—and he's found! Where? [*He takes a torch from a page's hand.*] Behold the sleepwalker on the bench down there, where the moonlight led him, fast asleep—though you never wanted to believe that he does such things! Look at him! See how preoccupied he is with dreams of his own future as he winds himself a splendid wreath of glory.

ELECTOR: How ridiculous!

HOHENZOLLERN: It's true! Just look: there he sits!

[*He shines the light upon the Prince from the ramp.*]

ELECTOR: Deep in sleep? It's not possible.

HOHENZOLLERN: Fast asleep. If you call out his name, he'll fall right down.

[*Pause*]

ELECTRESS: The young man must be very ill.

NATALIA: He needs a doctor.

ELECTRESS: I think we ought to help him and not waste time making fun of him.

HOHENZOLLERN [*handing back the torch*]: My dear compassionate ladies! He is quite well. By God, he's no less healthy than I am myself—as the Swedes will find out tomorrow on the battlefield. Believe me, his conduct is nothing more than a passing aberration of the mind.

ELECTOR: Good God—and I thought you were making it all up! Follow me, my friends! Let's have a closer look at him.

[*They descend the ramp.*]

COURTIER [*to the pages*]: Keep the torches away!

HOHENZOLLERN: Leave them where they are, it doesn't matter! The whole place could go up in flames and his mind would be no more aware of it than the diamond sparkling on his finger.

[*They surround him. The pages raise their torches.*]

ELECTOR [*bending over him*]: What kind of leaves are those he's twining? Willow branches?

HOHENZOLLERN: Willow! Good heavens, no, Excellency! It's laurel—like the wreaths he's seen on heroes' portraits in the armory in Berlin.

ELECTOR: Where could he have found such a bush in the sandy soil of my Brandenburg?

HOHENZOLLERN: God only knows.

COURTIER: Perhaps in the garden in back of the castle where the gardener cultivates all kinds of exotic plants.

ELECTOR: My word, how really strange this is. Well, in any case, the important thing is to find out what's occupying this young fool's mind.

HOHENZOLLERN: What else? Tomorrow's battle, Your Excellency! I'd like to bet he's seeing heavenly fortunetellers weaving him a crown of shining suns for his victory wreath.

[*The Prince looks at the wreath.*]

COURTIER: He's finished now.

HOHENZOLLERN: It's really too bad we don't have a mirror

here. I'm sure he'd walk up to it and try on the wreath, as vain as any girl, tilting it this way and that like a flowered hat.

ELECTOR: By God, I must see how far he'll go.

[*The Elector takes the wreath out of his hands. The Prince blushes and stares at him. The Elector then winds his chain of office around the wreath and gives it to the Princess. The Prince stands up in agitation. The Elector retreats with the Princess, who holds up the wreath. The Prince follows her with outstretched arms.*]

PRINCE [*whispering*]: Natalia! My darling! My bride!

ELECTOR: Hurry! Let's get away from him!

HOHENZOLLERN: What did the fool say?

COURTIER: What were his words?

[*They all go up the ramp.*]

PRINCE: Friedrich! My Prince! My father!

HOHENZOLLERN: Damn it all!

ELECTOR [*retreating backward*]: Just open the door!

PRINCE: Oh, mother!

HOHENZOLLERN: The madman! He is . . .

ELECTRESS: Whom is he calling "mother"?

PRINCE [*reaching for the wreath*]: Oh, my dearest! Why are you drawing back from me? Natalia!

[*He snatches a glove from the Princess's hand.*]

HOHENZOLLERN: Good God! What did he take?

COURTIER: The wreath?

NATALIA: No, no!

HOHENZOLLERN [*opening the door*]: Here, Your Majesty, quickly! Come inside! Let this whole tableau suddenly vanish from his sight!

ELECTOR: Back into the darkness with you, Prince of Homburg! Into nothingness! Nothingness! If it suits your convenience, we'll meet again upon the field of battle. The things you seek cannot be won by dreaming.
[*They all leave. The door clangs shut in the Prince's face. Pause.*]

SCENE 2

[*For a moment the Prince stands silently in front of the door with an expression of bewilderment on his face. Deep in thought, he then goes down the ramp, the hand holding Natalia's glove pressed against his forehead. When he reaches the bottom, he turns around and looks up again at the door.*]

SCENE 3

[*Count Hohenzollern enters from below through a garden gate. He is followed by a page. The Prince.*]

PAGE [*softly*]: Count, please listen! I implore you, Your Excellency!

HOHENZOLLERN [*annoyed*]: Be quiet, you chatterbox! What is it?

PAGE: I've been sent by . . .

HOHENZOLLERN: Don't wake him up with your babbling!

PAGE: The Elector has sent me here. He commands you not to breathe one word to the Prince when he wakes up, not a single word about the joke that His Majesty has just allowed himself to play.

HOHENZOLLERN [*quietly*]: He didn't need to tell me that! Be off with you! Go lie down in the wheatfield and take a nap!

[*The page leaves.*]

SCENE 4

[*Count Hohenzollern and the Prince.*]

HOHENZOLLERN [*placing himself slightly behind the Prince, who continues to stare fixedly up at the castle door*]: Arthur!

[*The Prince collapses.*]

HOHENZOLLERN: There he lies! A bullet couldn't have done a better job! [*He approaches the Prince.*] Now I am curious to see just what kind of excuse he'll invent to explain why he fell asleep here. [*He bends over the Prince.*] Arthur! Are you crazy? What are you doing here? How did you get to this place in the middle of the night?

PRINCE: Oh . . .

HOHENZOLLERN: Do you realize that your cavalry has already been on the march for an hour while you . . . you lie about in the garden and go to sleep.

PRINCE: What cavalry?

HOHENZOLLERN: The Mamelukes! Can it really be that he no

longer even knows that he commands the cavalry of Brandenburg?

PRINCE [*standing up*]: Quick! My helmet! My armor!

HOHENZOLLERN: Well, where are they?

PRINCE: Over there to your right . . . on the footstool.

HOHENZOLLERN: Where? On what stool?

PRINCE: Well, I thought I put them . . .

HOHENZOLLERN [*looking at him intently*]: So go and get them from the stool.

PRINCE: Whose glove is this? [*He contemplates the glove he is holding in his hand.*]

HOHENZOLLERN: How should I know? [*To himself*] Damn it all. He must have snatched the glove from the arm of the Princess without her noticing it. [*Abruptly*] You must hurry now. What are you waiting for? You must leave!

PRINCE [*throwing the glove down*]: Right away! Hey, Franz! That scoundrel was supposed to wake me up.

HOHENZOLLERN [*observing him*]: He's gone quite mad!

PRINCE: I swear, my dear Heinrich, I don't know where I am.

HOHENZOLLERN: In Fehrbellin, you distracted dreamer, in one of the side paths of the garden which lies behind the castle.

PRINCE [*to himself*]: If only night would swallow me! Once again I've been sleepwalking in the moonlight without knowing it. [*He pulls himself together.*] Forgive me. Now I remember what happened. The heat, you know, made it quite impossible for me to stay in bed last night. And so, since I was utterly exhausted, I crept into this garden here where Night herself embraced me like a lover. Her hair hung heavy with fragrance, and it was upon her lap I laid my head, like a bridegroom on his Persian bride's. What time is it now?

HOHENZOLLERN: Eleven-thirty.

PRINCE: And the squadrons have already set off, you say?

HOHENZOLLERN: Of course! At ten o'clock according to the plan. The Princess of Orange's regiment, leading the way, has doubtless already reached the heights of Hackelberg, where tomorrow morning it is to protect the army's secret advance against General Wrangel.

PRINCE: It doesn't matter that I'm not with them. Old Kottwitz is in command, and he knows the strategy down to every last detail. And in any case I would have had to return to headquarters here at two A.M., since we are to receive our final orders here. So it's just as well I stayed behind in Fehrbellin. Come, let's go. The Elector doesn't know anything of this, does he?

HOHENZOLLERN: Of course not. He's been long in bed asleep.

[*They are about to leave. The Prince hesitates, turns around, and picks up the glove.*]

PRINCE: What a strange dream I had! It was as if a royal castle all shimmering in gold and silver suddenly opened wide its doors. From high above, on the castle's marble ramp, a circle of those people dearest to my heart descended toward me as I watched—the Elector, the Electress, and some third person— now, what's her name?

HOHENZOLLERN: Who?

PRINCE [*He seems to be searching his memory.*]: She . . . the one I mean! Even a deaf mute would know her name.

HOHENZOLLERN: Lady Platen?

PRINCE: Of course not, my friend.

HOHENZOLLERN: Madame Ramin?

PRINCE: No, definitely not.

HOHENZOLLERN: Lady Bork? Or the Winterfeld woman?

PRINCE: No, no, I beg you! You seem unable to distinguish the pearl from its setting!

HOHENZOLLERN: Well, then, out with it! Is there a solution to this riddle? Which lady do you mean?

PRINCE: It doesn't matter! It doesn't matter! The name has slipped my mind now that I'm awake. Besides, it's irrelevant to what I'm telling you.

HOHENZOLLERN: Fine. Then, please continue.

PRINCE: But don't interrupt me! The Elector, with a brow like Zeus, held a wreath of laurel in his hand. He stood directly in front of me and, as if he wanted to set the very depths of my soul on fire, he wound his chain of office around the wreath and handed it over to someone else to place upon my head.

HOHENZOLLERN: To whom?

PRINCE: Oh, God!

HOHENZOLLERN: So speak!

PRINCE: Well, it was probably Lady Platen.

HOHENZOLLERN: Platen? Impossible! Isn't she in Prussia now?

PRINCE: It was Platen. Really. Or, maybe Madame Ramin.

HOHENZOLLERN: So, Madame Ramin! You don't say . . . with her red hair. Or Lady Platen with her teasing violet eyes. Everyone knows you like her.

PRINCE: I do like her.

HOHENZOLLERN: Well . . . and she, you say, held out the wreath to you?

PRINCE: Yes, like a goddess of fame and glory. She raised the wreath upon which the Elector's chain still dangled as if she intended to crown a hero. Filled with inexpressible emotion, I reached out to seize it; I wanted to sink upon my knees before her. But just as the mist, which hovers in a valley, is dispersed by the first fresh breath of wind, so this group of people retreated from me, and climbed back up the ramp. And when I tried to climb it too, the path stretched out endlessly before me . . . right up to the gates of heaven. Reaching out anxiously to all sides, I tried to grasp hold of one of these dear friends. In vain. The castle's door suddenly opened, and a flash of lightning burst forth, consuming them. With that, the door slammed shut again with a great roar. But in my violent pursuit, I did manage to snatch a glove from the arm of my lovely dream-image. And when I awoke, good God! . . . I was holding a glove in my hand.

HOHENZOLLERN: And do you mean to say this glove is hers?

PRINCE: Whose?

HOHENZOLLERN: Well, Platen's.

PRINCE: Yes, Platen's. Really. Or Ramin's.

HOHENZOLLERN [*laughing*]: You are a sly devil with your visions. I'd like to know what kind of secret rendezvous in flesh and blood really took place here from which this glove remained a souvenir!

PRINCE: What are you saying? If you think that I . . . ! I swear by my true love . . . !

HOHENZOLLERN: Well, it's none of my business. For all I care, your phantom can be Platen or Ramin! The mail coach leaves for Prussia on Sunday, so you can find out right away whether your lovely lady is missing a glove. Let's go. It's twelve o'clock. Why are we standing here talking?

PRINCE [*in a dreamlike state*]: You're right! Let's go to bed. But just a moment—what I wanted to ask, dear friend—are the

Electress and her niece still here, the charming Princess of Orange who's just arrived at headquarters?

HOHENZOLLERN: Why? I do believe, the fool . . .

PRINCE: Why? You know I'm supposed to have thirty men escort them from the battle zone. I've had to ask Captain Ramin to take care of this.

HOHENZOLLERN: They're long since gone . . . or, are just about to leave. Ramin, completely prepared for his departure, stood all night long at the gates. But let's go at once! It's twelve, and I'd like to rest a little before the battle starts.

[*They both leave.*]

SCENE 5

Scene: Fehrbellin. A room in the castle. Shots are heard in the distance.

[*The Electress and Princess Natalia in traveling clothes, escorted by a courtier, enter and sit down at the side. Ladies-in-waiting. Enter the Elector, Field Marshal Dörfling, the Prince of Homburg with his glove tucked into his coat, Count Hohenzollern, Count Truchss, Colonel Hennings, Cavalry Captain von der Goltz, and several other generals, colonels, and officers.*]

ELECTOR: Where's the shooting coming from? Is it Götz?

FIELD MARSHAL: Yes, Your Majesty, it's Colonel Götz, who moved forward with the advance guard yesterday. He's already sent back an officer to set your mind at rest about the military situation. A Swedish outpost of a thousand men has advanced as far as the Hackelberg; but Götz is certain he can hold these hills and assures me that you can carry on as if they were already occupied.

ELECTOR [*to the officers*]: Gentlemen! Field Marshal Dörfling knows the battle plan. Take out your pens, please, and write it down.

[*The officers gather around the Field Marshal and take out their notebooks.*]

ELECTOR [*turning to the courtier*]: Has Captain Ramin come yet with the coach?

COURTIER: He'll be right here, Your Majesty! The horses are being harnessed now.

ELECTOR [*sitting down on a chair behind the Electress and the Princess*]: Ramin will escort my dear Elizabeth, and thirty brave cavalrymen will follow him. You and Natalia will go to my chancellor's castle near Havelberg. It's on the other side of the Havel River where no more Swedes will dare to let themselves be seen.

ELECTRESS: Is the ferry running again?

ELECTOR: Near Havelberg? Arrangements have been made. In any case, it'll be daylight before you reach the crossing. [*Pause*] But Natalia is so quiet. What's bothering my sweet child?

NATALIA: I'm afraid, dear uncle.

ELECTOR: And yet my little daughter is no less safe now than she was in her mother's arms.

[*Pause*]

ELECTRESS: When do you think we'll meet again?

ELECTOR: When God grants me victory, as He doubtless will . . . perhaps in the course of the next day or so.

[*Pages come and serve breakfast to the ladies. Field Marshal Dörfling dictates. The Prince of Homburg, pen and notebook in hand, stares fixedly at the ladies.*]

FIELD MARSHAL: Gentlemen, the purpose of His Majesty's battle plan is to scatter the fleeing Swedish army and separate it from its bridgehead on the Rhyn which protects it from behind. Colonel Hennings . . .

HENNINGS: Here! [*He writes.*]

FIELD MARSHAL: . . . whom His Majesty has ordered to take command of the right flank of our army, is to try to circle secretly around the enemy's left wing in the Hackel Valley so as to thrust himself boldly in between the Swedes and their three bridges. Then, joining up with Count Truchss . . . Count Truchss!

TRUCHSS: Here! [*He writes.*]

FIELD MARSHAL: . . . joining up with Count Truchss . . . [*He pauses.*] who in the meanwhile has taken up a position in the mountains opposite Wrangel . . .

TRUCHSS [*writing*]: "taken up a position . . ."

FIELD MARSHAL: Do you have that? [*He continues.*] . . . Hennings will try to drive the Swedes into the swamp which lies behind their right flank.

GUARD [*dressed as a Hungarian foot soldier*]: The carriage has just arrived.

[*The ladies rise.*]

FIELD MARSHAL: The Prince of Homburg . . .

ELECTOR [*also rising*]: Is Captain Ramin ready?

GUARD: He's already mounted and waiting at the door.

[*The Elector, the Electress, and Natalia take leave from one another.*]

TRUCHSS [*writing*]: "which lies behind their right flank."

FIELD MARSHAL: The Prince of Homburg . . . Where is the Prince of Homburg?

HOHENZOLLERN [*whispering*]: Arthur!

PRINCE [*with a start*]: Here!

HOHENZOLLERN: Have you lost your senses?

PRINCE: What does the Field Marshal command? [*He blushes, takes up his pen and notebook, and writes.*]

FIELD MARSHAL: . . . whom His Majesty has once again entrusted to command with honor all of Brandenburg's cavalry—as once before at Rathenau—of course, without forgetting Colonel Kottwitz, who will stay by his side and render him assistance . . . [*Softly to Goltz*] Is Kottwitz here?

GOLTZ: No, General, as you can see. He's sent me in his place to get our orders straight from you.

[*The Prince looks at the ladies again.*]

FIELD MARSHAL [*continuing*]: . . . will station himself on the plains near the village of Hackelwitz opposite the right wing of the army and beyond the cannon's range.

GOLTZ [*writing*]: "beyond the cannon's range."

[*The Electress wraps a scarf around the Princess's neck. The Princess, as she wants to put on her gloves, turns around as if looking for something.*]

ELECTOR [*stepping toward her*]: My daughter, what's wrong?

ELECTRESS: Are you looking for something?

PRINCESS: I don't know, dear aunt, my glove . . .

ELECTOR [*to the ladies-in-waiting*]: Lovely ladies! Would you be so kind and help?

ELECTRESS [*to the Princess*]: You have it in your hand, child!

NATALIA: I have the right glove, but where's the left one?

ELECTRESS: Perhaps you left it in your bedroom.

NATALIA: Oh, Lady Bork, would you mind looking?

ELECTOR [*to Lady Bork*]: Hurry, quickly!

NATALIA: Look on the mantlepiece!

[*Lady Bork leaves.*]

PRINCE [*to himself*]: My God! Did I hear correctly? [*He takes the glove out of his collar.*]

FIELD MARSHAL [*looking at the papers which he is holding in his hands*]: . . . beyond the cannon's range. [*He continues.*] His Highness, the Prince . . .

PRINCE: The glove, she's looking for the glove! [*He looks back and forth, first at the glove and then at the Princess.*]

FIELD MARSHAL: in accordance with our Sovereign's express command . . .

GOLTZ [*writing*]: "in accordance with our Sovereign's express command . . ."

FIELD MARSHAL: . . . is not to move from the place assigned to him, whatever course the battle takes . . .

PRINCE: Now, quick! I must find out if this glove belongs to her. [*He drops the glove together with his handkerchief and then picks up the handkerchief, leaving the glove where everyone can see it.*]

FIELD MARSHAL [*in dismay*]: What is His Highness, the Prince, doing?

HOHENZOLLERN [*whispering*]: Arthur!

PRINCE: Here!

HOHENZOLLERN: Have you lost your senses?

PRINCE: What are my Field Marshal's orders? [*He picks up his notebook and pen again. The Field Marshal casts a brief questioning look at him.*]

GOLTZ [*after having finished writing*]: "is not to move from the place assigned to him . . ."

FIELD MARSHAL [*continuing*]: . . . until the moment when, pressed by Hennings and Truchss . . .

PRINCE [*whispering to Goltz while looking at the notebook*]: Who? Goltz, my dear fellow! What? I?

GOLTZ: You, yes! Of course, who else?

PRINCE: I'm not to move from the place assigned . . . ?

GOLTZ: Exactly!

FIELD MARSHAL: Well? Do you have it?

PRINCE [*aloud*]: "is not to move from the place assigned to him . . ." [*He writes.*]

FIELD MARSHAL: . . . until the moment when . . . [*He pauses.*] . . . the enemy's left flank has been dispursed by Hennings and Truchss and forced upon its own right wing so that the entire Swedish army can only totter backward toward the plains. In accordance with the battle plan, it is there, in the ditch-riddled swamps, that the Swedes are to be annihilated.

ELECTOR: Pages, light the way! My arm, ladies! [*He leaves with the Electress and the Princess.*]

FIELD MARSHAL: At that moment, the Elector will sound a fanfare.

ELECTRESS [*to a few officers who bow to her*]: Goodbye, gentlemen! Don't let us disturb you.

[*The Field Marshal also bows.*]

ELECTOR [*stopping suddenly*]: Look! The Princess's glove. Quickly, it's lying over there!

COURTIER: Where?

ELECTOR: At the feet of our cousin, the Prince of Homburg!

PRINCE [*gallantly*]: At my feet? What? Is that your glove? [*He picks it up and brings it to the Princess.*]

NATALIA: I thank you, noble Prince.

PRINCE [*confused*]: Is that your glove?

NATALIA: Yes, it's mine, the one I lost. [*She takes it and puts it on.*]

ELECTRESS [*to the Prince as she leaves*]: Farewell, farewell! Good luck and God be with you! See to it that we'll be reunited soon.

[*The Elector leaves with the two ladies, followed by ladies-in-waiting, courtiers, and pages.*]

PRINCE [*He stands still for a moment as if struck by lightning, then strides back triumphantly and returns to the circle of officers.*]: "At that moment, the Elector will sound a fanfare." [*He pretends to write.*]

FIELD MARSHAL [*looking at his orders*]: At that moment, the Elector will sound a fanfare. However, in order to prevent a premature attack upon the enemy through some misunderstanding . . .

GOLTZ [*writing*]: "a premature attack upon the enemy through some misunderstanding . . ."

PRINCE [*In a state of great agitation, he whispers to Hohenzollern.*]: Oh, Heinrich!

HOHENZOLLERN [*annoyed*]: Well, what is it? What do you want now?

PRINCE: What? Did you see nothing?

HOHENZOLLERN: No, nothing! Be still, damn it all!

FIELD MARSHAL [*continuing*]: His Majesty, the Elector, will send an officer from his suite to bring you an express order to attack. Now note this carefully, the fanfare will *not* be sounded before the messenger has arrived.

[*The Prince stands daydreaming.*]

FIELD MARSHAL: Have you written that down?

GOLTZ [*writing*]: "The fanfare will *not* be sounded before the messenger has arrived."

FIELD MARSHAL [*raising his voice*]: Your Highness, have you written that down?

PRINCE: Excuse me, Field Marshal?

FIELD MARSHAL: Have you written that down?

PRINCE: About the fanfare?

HOHENZOLLERN [*whispering in annoyance and with emphasis*]: Fanfare be damned! *Not until* the messenger . . .

GOLTZ: Not until he . . .

PRINCE [*interrupting them*]: Yes, of course! Not until . . . but then he'll let the fanfare sound. [*He writes. Pause.*]

FIELD MARSHAL: Baron Goltz, please write this down. I would like to speak to Colonel Kottwitz personally before the beginning of the battle, if it is at all possible.

GOLTZ [*comprehending the Field Marshal's meaning*]: I will see to it, rest assured.

[*Pause.*]

ELECTOR [*returning*]: Well, my generals and officers. The dawn is breaking. Have you finished taking notes?

FIELD MARSHAL: We have finished, Your Majesty. Your battle plan has been conveyed to all your officers point for point.

ELECTOR [*taking his hat and gloves*]: Prince of Homburg, to you I must urge calmness and composure. In the recent past, as you well know, you have already cost me two battles along the banks of the Rhine. So keep yourself in check and see to it that you don't cause me to lose a third one today. For nothing less than my throne and realm depend on this battle's outcome. [*To the officers*] Follow me! Hey, Franz!

GROOM [*entering*]: Here!

ELECTOR: Quickly, bring my horse! I want to be on the battle-field before the sun is up.

[*The Elector leaves, followed by generals, colonels, and other officers.*]

SCENE 6

PRINCE [*stepping into the foreground*]: Now, roll on, oh mighty wheel of fortune! As a breath of wind billows out the sails of ships, oh goddess, lift back your veils for me! Smiling, you have already touched me once today and, passing by, threw me a pledge of favor from your horn of plenty. I will look for you today, oh fickle daughter of the gods, and I will catch you on the field of battle. There I will turn your cornucopia upside down and spread its blessings at my feet. And even if you should be bound with seven iron chains to the Swedish chariots of victory, I shall possess you! [*He leaves.*]

CURTAIN

Act II

SCENE 1

Scene: The battlefield near Fehrbellin.

[*Colonel Kottwitz, Count Hohenzollern, Cavalry Captain von der Goltz, and other officers arrive at the head of the cavalry.*]

KOTTWITZ [*from off stage*]: Halt the cavalry here and dismount!

HOHENZOLLERN AND GOLTZ [*entering*]: Halt! Halt!

KOTTWITZ [*from off stage*]: Which of my friends will help me to dismount?

HOHENZOLLERN AND GOLTZ: I will, old comrade, I will. [*They leave the stage again.*]

KOTTWITZ [*from off stage*]: Thank you! Uff! A plague on these old bones. I hope that some day when you are falling apart you'll have a noble son to help you as you've helped me. [*He enters followed by Hohenzollern, Goltz, and others.*] Ah, yes! Seated on my horse I feel full of youthful vigor. But when I get off, a raging battle starts inside me as if my body and soul were wrenching themselves apart. [*He looks around.*] Where is our commander, His Highness, the Prince of Homburg?

HOHENZOLLERN: The Prince will be with you shortly.

KOTTWITZ: Where is he?

HOHENZOLLERN: He rode into the village that lay hidden behind the bushes to the side of the road. He'll be back right away.

OFFICER: I hear he took a tumble from his horse last night.

HOHENZOLLERN: Yes, I believe that's true.

KOTTWITZ: He fell?

HOHENZOLLERN: It was nothing serious. His horse shied at a windmill, but the Prince slid gently off to the side and didn't injure himself in the least. It's not worth a second thought.

KOTTWITZ [*going up a small hill*]: It is a truly beautiful day, by heaven! A day created by God, the great Ruler of the Universe, for gentler things than war. As the sun glimmers red behind the clouds, one's feelings soar joyously upward, like the lark, into the calm and fragrant skies.

GOLTZ: Have you met up with Marshal Dörfling yet?

KOTTWITZ [*stepping forward*]: Damn it, no! What does His Excellency expect? Am I an arrow, a bird, a thought that he can shoot me across the whole battlefield? First I was with the advance guard on the heights of Hackelberg, and then I rode back to bring up the rear as we marched through the Hackel Valley. But the one person I could not find was the Field Marshal himself! So I looked for my own troops and rejoined them.

GOLTZ: He will be very sorry to have missed you. Apparently he had something important to confide in you.

OFFICER: Here comes His Highness, the Prince, our commander.

SCENE 2

[*Enter the Prince of Homburg with his left hand bandaged in a black cloth.*]

KOTTWITZ: Greetings, my young and noble Prince. Take a look and see how I have deployed the cavalry along the valley road while you were in the village. I think you'll be satisfied with me.

PRINCE: Good morning, Kottwitz. Good morning, friends. You know I always approve of everything you do.

HOHENZOLLERN: Arthur, what have you been doing in the village? You look so serious.

PRINCE: I? . . . I was in the chapel which I saw glittering in the sunlight, half hidden behind the village hedges. As we were passing by, the bells were ringing for morning prayers, and I was seized by an urge to throw myself upon my knees before the altar.

KOTTWITZ: A pious young man, I must say! Believe me, a task that begins with prayers will be crowned with blessings, fame, and victory.

PRINCE: I wanted to ask you something, Heinrich . . . [*He walks forward a few steps with Count Hohenzollern.*] What was it again that Dörfling read out at last night's general staff meeting about my orders for today?

HOHENZOLLERN: You were distracted. I certainly noticed that.

PRINCE: Distracted . . . divided, I don't know what was wrong with me. I get confused when I have to take dictation.

HOHENZOLLERN: Fortunately, there wasn't much for you to

27

note. Truchss and Hennings who are in command of the foot soldiers have been assigned to attack the enemy. You have been ordered to remain here in the valley, holding the cavalry in readiness until you've been sent an order to attack.

PRINCE [*after a pause, in which he appears to have fallen into a daydream*]: A strange occurrence!

HOHENZOLLERN: What is, my friend? [*He looks at him. A cannon shot is heard.*]

KOTTWITZ: Hurray, my Lords, hurray! Mount your horses! That was Hennings, and the battle has begun.

[*They all climb a hill.*]

PRINCE: Who is it? What?

HOHENZOLLERN: Colonel Hennings, Arthur, who has crept in behind Wrangel's rear guard. Just come along, you can watch everything from the hilltop.

GOLTZ [*standing on the hill*]: See how formidable our troops look spread out along the Rhyn.

PRINCE [*shading his eyes with his hand*]: Is that Hennings over there near our right wing?

FIRST OFFICER: Yes, Your Excellency!

PRINCE: What does this mean, damn it! His position yesterday was to the left.

[*Cannon shot is heard in the distance.*]

KOTTWITZ: Damn it all! Wrangel's now directed all twelve of his cannon at Henning's soldiers.

FIRST OFFICER: The Swedes are well entrenched, I must say!

SECOND OFFICER: By God, their fortifications rise nearly as high as the spire of the village church behind them.

[*Shots are heard nearby.*]

GOLTZ: That is Truchss.

PRINCE: Truchss?

KOTTWITZ: Yes, Truchss. He's coming to Henning's aid from the front.

PRINCE: How come Truchss has ended up in the center today?

[*Violent cannon shots*]

GOLTZ: Good God, look! I think the town has caught on fire!

THIRD OFFICER: It *is* burning!

FIRST OFFICER: It's burning! It's burning! The flames have already reached the tower.

GOLTZ: My God, the Swedish couriers are flying right and left!

SECOND OFFICER: The troops are retreating.

KOTTWITZ: Where?

FIRST OFFICER: On the right flank.

THIRD OFFICER: Yes, their columns are moving. Three regiments of men! It looks like they want to strengthen the left flank.

SECOND OFFICER: So it seems. And the cavalry is advancing to cover the new deployment of the right wing.

HOHENZOLLERN [*laughing*]: Ha! How they will go running from the field again when they catch sight of us lying hidden here in the valley!

[*Musket fire*]

KOTTWITZ: Look, comrades, look!

SECOND OFFICER: And listen!

29

FIRST OFFICER: It's musket fire!

THIRD OFFICER: Our troops have met the enemy at the trenches!

GOLTZ: By God. I've never in all my life heard such cannon thunder.

HOHENZOLLERN: Shoot! Shoot! Make the womb of the earth split open and may the scar serve as a monument to your dead!

[*Pause. A cry of victory is heard in the distance.*]

FIRST OFFICER: Thanks be to God who's granted us this victory! Wrangel is already retreating.

HOHENZOLLERN: No, it cannot be!

GOLTZ: Yes, my friends, he's leaving! Look at the left flank. He's taking the cannon and abandoning the fortifications.

ALL: Triumph! Triumph! Triumph! The victory is ours!

PRINCE [*coming down the hill*]: Come, Kottwitz, follow me!

KOTTWITZ: Be calm, my children, be calm!

PRINCE: Let's go! Sound the fanfare! Follow me!

KOTTWITZ: Be calm, I tell you!

PRINCE [*wildly*]: Heaven, earth, and hell!

KOTTWITZ: At the general staff meeting yesterday, His Highness gave us orders not to move until commanded. Goltz, read this gentleman the orders.

PRINCE: Wait until commanded? Oh, Kottwitz, are you such a slow rider then? Haven't you ever received orders from your heart?

KOTTWITZ: Orders?

HOHENZOLLERN: I beg you, gentlemen!

KOTTWITZ: From my heart?

HOHENZOLLERN: Listen to reason, Arthur!

GOLTZ: Listen, my Colonel.

KOTTWITZ [*offended*]: Oho! So that's the way I strike you, my young master! Well, should it come to it, I could drag your horse behind me by the tail. On the march, gentlemen! Trumpeters, sound the fanfare! On to battle! To battle! Kottwitz is here!

GOLTZ [*to Kottwitz*]: No, absolutely not, my Colonel. Absolutely not!

SECOND OFFICER: Hennings has not yet reached the Rhyn.

FIRST OFFICER: Take his sword.

PRINCE: My sword? [*He shoves him back.*] You impertinent boy! Don't you even know the ten commandments of the Brandenburg army yet? It's your sword I'll take, together with its sheath! [*He tears the sword from the officer's side along with its belt.*]

FIRST OFFICER [*reeling*]: My Prince, your action, by God . . . !

PRINCE [*striding toward him*]: You dare to open your mouth?

HOHENZOLLERN [*to the officer*]: Be quiet! Are you crazy?

PRINCE [*giving the sword to another officer*]: Orderlies! Take this man away to prison at our headquarters! [*To Kottwitz and the other officers*] And now, gentlemen, here are your new orders! A soldier who does not follow his general into battle is a cowardly scoundrel! Well . . . and which of you are staying behind?

KOTTWITZ: You heard my answer. Why are you getting so upset?

HOHENZOLLERN [*soothingly to the Prince*]: They were only giving you advice.

KOTTWITZ: I'll follow you, but be it on your own head!

PRINCE [*calmed*]: Let it be upon my head. Follow me, my brothers!

[*They all leave.*]

SCENE 3

Scene: Room in a village house.

[*A courtier in boots and spurs enters. A peasant and his wife are seated at a table, working.*]

COURTIER: Greetings, good people! Do you have room in your house for a few guests?

PEASANT: Of course, gladly.

PEASANT'S WIFE: May one know for whom?

COURTIER: For the first lady of the land, no less. The axle of her coach broke at the village gate, and since we've learned that the battle is already over, we no longer need to continue on our way.

BOTH [*standing up*]: The battle is over?

COURTIER: You didn't know that? The Swedish army has been defeated and Brandenburg is safe from sword and fire . . . if not forever, then at least for one year's time. But look! Here comes Her Majesty herself.

SCENE 4

[*The Electress, pale and distraught; Princess Natalia and several ladies follow. The others.*]

ELECTRESS [*standing on the threshold*]: Bork! Winterfeld! Come, give me your arm!

NATALIA [*hurrying toward her*]: My dearest mother!

LADIES-IN-WAITING: God! She's turning white. She's fainting! [*They support her.*]

ELECTRESS: Find me a chair, I must sit down. Dead, did he say, dead?

NATALIA: My dearest mother!

ELECTRESS: I want to speak with the messenger of doom myself!

SCENE 5

[*Cavalry Captain von Mörner, who is wounded, enters on the arm of two cavalrymen. The above.*]

ELECTRESS: What news do you bring me, dreadful messenger?

MÖRNER: Unfortunately, only what my eyes themselves have seen, dear Lady, to my eternal grief.

ELECTRESS: Let me hear it all.

MÖRNER: The Elector is no more.

NATALIA: Oh, God! Must such a terrible blow strike us now? [*She covers her face.*]

ELECTRESS: I want to know exactly how he fell. So let your report be like a flash of lightning that illuminates the world in one last purple glow as it strikes the wanderer in his path. And after you have spoken, may night come crashing down upon my head.

MÖRNER [*Accompanied by the two cavalrymen, he steps in front of her.*]: The Prince of Homburg had advanced against Wrangel on the plains as soon as the Swedish position began to weaken under attack by Truchss. He had just managed to break through two enemy lines with his cavalry and destroy the troops in flight when he stumbled upon Swedish field artillery. He was pounded by such a murderous rain of shells that his men went down like wheat beneath a storm, and he had to halt between some hills and bushes to reassemble his scattered forces.

NATALIA [*to the Electress*]: Oh, my dearest! Take courage!

ELECTRESS: Let me be, my dear!

MÖRNER: Just then we saw our Sovereign emerging from a cloud of dust and ride toward the enemy, surrounded by Colonel Truchss's battle standards. Radiantly, he sat there on his horse bathed in the sun's brilliant rays as if lighting up our path to victory. Regrouping ourselves on a hilltop, we were most distraught to see him in the middle of the bombardment. And then, before our very eyes, His Majesty, both horse and rider, collapsed and fell to the ground. Two standard bearers threw themselves over him and covered him with their flags.

NATALIA: Oh, my dearest mother.

FIRST LADY-IN-WAITING: Oh, heavens!

ELECTRESS: Continue! Continue!

MÖRNER: The Prince, seeing this horrifying spectacle, was seized with anguish beyond words. Bursting with fùry like a wild bear and driven by revenge, he charged toward the Swedish trenches, taking us with him. Thus he stormed the enemy's fortifications, scattered and destroyed their troops on the battlefield, and brought back as booty all the cannons, flags, and drums and standards . . . in a word, the entire Swedish military equipment. And if it had not been for the bridgehead on the Rhyn, not a single Swedish soldier would have been left alive to sit at his hearth and tell his children how he saw the heroic Elector of Brandenburg fall near Fehrbellin!

ELECTRESS: This victory of ours was purchased at too dear a price, and I don't want it. Give me back the price you paid. [*She faints.*]

FIRST LADY-IN-WAITING: Help! She's fainted.

[*Natalia weeps.*]

SCENE 6

[*The Prince of Homburg enters. The above.*]

PRINCE: Oh, my dearest Natalia! [*With deep emotion, he places her hand upon his heart.*]

NATALIA: So, it's true then?

PRINCE: Oh, if I could only say it is not true. If I could only bring him back to life again with the blood of my own loyal heart.

NATALIA [*drying her tears*]: Has his body been found yet?

PRINCE: Until this moment, all my energies went into taking

revenge against Wrangel. Where was I to find time for this other task? However, I've just now sent out a detachment of men to find our Sovereign on the field of death. I have no doubt the body will be returned to us before the sun goes down.

NATALIA: Who will now hold back the Swedish army in this monstrous war? Who will protect us from the whole world of enemies which his fame and good fortune have roused against us?

PRINCE [*taking her hand*]: I, dear Lady, will take on the responsibility. Like an angel with a flaming sword, I will stand beside your throne now deserted by His Majesty's death. The Elector intended to free Brandenburg before the end of this year. Very well! I shall be the executor of his last wish.

NATALIA: My dear and noble cousin! [*She withdraws her hand.*]

PRINCE: Natalia . . . [*He pauses a moment.*] How do you picture your future now?

NATALIA: Oh, what am I to do now that this storm has destroyed the ground beneath my feet? My father and my dearest mother are resting in their graves in Amsterdam while Dortrecht, my ancestral home, lies destroyed in ashes and in ruins. Maurice of Orange, my cousin, who is himself hard pressed by the Spanish tyrant's armies, scarcely knows how he is to rescue his own children from destruction. And now, the last support to my flowering hope has crumbled. Today I have been orphaned for the second time.

PRINCE [*putting his arm around her*]: My dear friend! Were the hour not consecrated to mourning, I would say: wind your fragrant branches around this heart which has beaten all these years in solitude, yearning for nothing but the sweet scent of your flowers.

NATALIA: My dear, good cousin.

PRINCE: Will you? Will you?

NATALIA: Will you allow me to take root in your deepest self? [*She leans upon him.*]

PRINCE: What? What was that you said?

NATALIA: Leave me!

PRINCE [*continuing to hold her*]: Yes, into the innermost core of my being, Natalia, into the inmost depths of my heart. [*He kisses her; she breaks away.*] Oh, God! If only he were here now, the man we mourn, to witness this union of ours. If only we could kneel to him in prayer and ask: Father, give us your blessings! [*He covers his face with his hands. Natalia turns back to the Electress.*]

SCENE 7

[*A sergeant rushes in. The above.*]

SERGEANT: My Prince, by the living God above us, I scarcely dare to report to you the rumor that is spreading: the Elector is alive.

PRINCE: He is alive?

SERGEANT: Count Sparren is coming with the news.

NATALIA: My God, mother, did you hear? [*She throws herself down before the Electress and embraces her.*]

PRINCE: No! Tell me . . . who's coming? . . .

SERGEANT: Count George von Sparren, who with his own eyes saw the Elector alive and well among Truchss's troops in Hackelwitz.

PRINCE: Quickly! Run, old man! Bring him here to me.

[*The sergeant leaves.*]

SCENE 8

[*Count von Sparren and the sergeant enter. The above.*]

ELECTRESS: Oh, do not plunge me a second time into the abyss!

NATALIA: No, my dear mother!

ELECTRESS: Friedrich is alive?

NATALIA [*supporting her with both hands*]: Now you may stand once again upon life's most joyous peaks.

SERGEANT [*stepping forward*]: Here is the officer.

PRINCE: Count von Sparren! So you've seen His Majesty alive and well in Hackelwitz with Truchss's troops?

SPARREN: Yes, my noble Prince, in the parson's courtyard where, surrounded by his staff, he was giving orders to bury the dead of both armies.

LADIES-IN-WAITING [*embracing*]: Oh, God!

ELECTRESS: My beloved daughter!

NATALIA: Such joy is almost too much to bear. [*She buries her head in her aunt's lap.*]

PRINCE: Didn't I myself from where I was standing at the head of my troops see him fall along with his horse? Wasn't he shattered by a rain of cannon shot?

SPARREN: It's true, the horse did fall along with its rider. But the man who rode it, my Prince, was not His Majesty.

PRINCE: Not him? Not His Majesty?

NATALIA: Oh, how wonderful! [*She rises and stands beside the Electress.*]

PRINCE: Speak! Tell us everything. Your words weigh heavy like gold upon my chest.

SPARREN: Listen to the most touching story you've ever heard. His Majesty, our leader, deaf to every warning once again insisted upon riding his gleaming white stallion—you know, the one which Froben recently brought back to him from England. And as usual, it was the target of all the enemy's bullets, so that not even one of those who belonged to his suite could get within a hundred paces of him. Bullets whizzed and grenades and shrapnel flew toward him like a veritable river of death, forcing everyone who was still alive to retreat beyond the borders of this destructive tide. Only he, the bold swimmer, did not waiver in his course and, nodding to his friends, he rowed calmly toward the heights from which this deadly river flowed.

PRINCE: Yes, indeed, it was a grisly sight!

SPARREN: Froben, the Elector's groom, who was the first to follow him, told me as he rode by: "Today I curse the brilliant gleam of this white horse, bought recently for so much gold in London. How gladly I'd give fifty ducats if I could hide it with a coat of mouselike gray." He approached him, feverish with worry, and said: "Majesty, your horse is nervous; you must permit me to take him back for further training!" With these words, Froben got off his own horse and took hold of the stallion's reigns, whereupon the Elector too dismounted and said with a quiet smile: "The tricks you wish to teach this horse, old fellow, cannot be learned as long as daylight lasts. I beg you, take him far away behind those hills where the enemy won't notice his defects!" Then the Elector mounted Froben's chestnut horse and returned to the duties which were calling him. But Froben had hardly mounted the white stallion when a murderous shot from the trenches brought him down—both horse and rider sank. And so he fell, a victim of his loyalty, and no one heard a further sound from him.

[*Short pause.*]

PRINCE: He's been well paid. If I'd been given ten lives, I couldn't use them for a better purpose.

NATALIA: Brave Froben.

ELECTRESS: Excellent man.

NATALIA: A far less deserving man would still be worthy of our tears.

[*They weep.*]

PRINCE: Enough of this. Now to business. Where is the Elector? Has he set up headquarters in Hackelwitz?

SPARREN: I beg your pardon, Prince. His Majesty has gone to Berlin and has requested the entire general staff to follow.

PRINCE: What? To Berlin? Is the battle over, then?

SPARREN: Good heavens, I'm amazed you don't know all of this. Count Horn, the Swedish envoy, has arrived and a cease-fire was called in all the camps. If I understood Field Marshal Dörfling correctly, negotiations have already begun from which peace itself could easily follow.

ELECTRESS: Oh, God! How wonderfully everything is turning out. [*She rises.*]

PRINCE: Come, let's follow him immediately to Berlin! Could you make room for me in your carriage to expedite my journey? I only have to write a word or two to Kottwitz, and then I'll join you in a moment. [*He sits down and writes.*]

ELECTRESS: Of course, I can. With all my heart.

PRINCE [*He folds the letter and gives it to the sergeant, then turns to the Electress while placing his arm gently about Natalia.*]: I still have one wish to confess to you and, shy though I feel about it, I would like to unburden myself to you on the trip.

NATALIA [*moving away from him*]: Bork! Quickly! My scarf, I beg you!

ELECTRESS: You? Have a request to make of me?

FIRST LADY-IN-WAITING: You are wearing the scarf, Princess, around your neck.

PRINCE [*to the Electress*]: What? Can't you guess?

ELECTRESS: No. Nothing.

PRINCE: Really? Not the slightest inkling?

ELECTRESS [*interrupting him*]: It doesn't matter! Today I couldn't deny a request from anyone on earth, no matter what it was. Least of all could I say no to you, the victor of today's battle. Let us go.

PRINCE: Oh, mother. How happy your words have made me. May I interpret them as I like?

ELECTRESS: Let's go, I say. We'll speak more of this in the carriage.

PRINCE: Come, give me your arm. Oh, divine Caesar! I shall attach my ladder to your star.

[*He leads the ladies away. Everyone follows.*]

SCENE 9

Scene: Berlin. A pleasure garden in front of the old castle. In the background, the castle church with a front staircase. Bells

*are ringing. The church is brightly illuminated. Froben's body
is being carried past and placed on a magnificent catafalque.*

[*The Elector, Field Marshal Dörfling, Colonel Hennings,
Count Truchss, and a few other colonels and officers enter.
Several officers with dispatches enter from the opposite side.
People of every age and sex are gathered in the church and
on the square.*]

ELECTOR: Whoever it was who led the cavalry on the day of
battle and arbitrarily advanced before I gave him orders to attack, forcing the enemy to retreat before Colonel Hennings
was able to destroy the bridges . . . whoever it may be, I say,
he has incurred the penalty of death, and I command that he
appear before a court-martial. The Prince of Homburg did not
lead the troops, you say?

TRUCHSS: No, Your Majesty.

ELECTOR: Who can confirm this?

TRUCHSS: Various cavalrymen who assured me of this even before the battle started. The Prince, it seems, had a fall from his
horse and suffered serious injuries to his head and legs. The
men themselves saw his wounds being treated in a church.

ELECTOR: Well, it doesn't matter. Today's victory was brilliant, and I will thank God for it tomorrow at the altar. But
even if it had been ten times greater, it would not exonerate
the person who procured it by mere chance. I have many more
battles than this one to win and demand obedience to the law.
Whoever it was who led the troops into battle, I repeat it once
again, has forfeited his head, and I hereby summon him to appear before a military court. Now, my friends, follow me into
the church!

SCENE 10

[*The Prince of Homburg enters carrying three Swedish flags. He is followed by Colonel Kottwitz with two flags, Count Hohenzollern, Cavalry Captain Goltz, and Count Reuss, each with a flag. Several other officers, corporals, and cavalrymen enter, all with flags. There are many drums and standards. The above.*]

DÖRFLING [*as soon as he catches sight of the Prince*]: The Prince of Homburg. Truchss!? What have you done?

ELECTOR [*amazed*]: Where have you come from, Prince?

PRINCE [*advancing a few steps*]: From Fehrbellin, my Lord, and bring you these trophies of victory.

[*He lays the flags down in front of the Elector. The officers, corporals, and cavalrymen follow suit, each with their own flags.*]

ELECTOR [*taken aback*]: I heard you were wounded . . . dangerously so, isn't that true? Count Truchss!

PRINCE [*cheerfully*]: I beg your pardon?

TRUCHUSS: By heaven, I'm amazed.

PRINCE: My horse fell at the beginning of the battle but this hand here, which the field surgeon bound, does not deserve to be called wounded.

ELECTOR: So, you led the cavalry then?

PRINCE [*looking at him*]: I? Of course! Do you have to hear this from me? I've just placed the proof at your feet.

ELECTOR: Take his sword. He is under arrest.

FIELD MARSHAL [*shocked*]: Whose sword?

ELECTOR [*stepping among the flags*]: Greetings, Kottwitz!

TRUCHSS [*to himself*]: Damn it!

KOTTWITZ: By God, I am utterly . . .

ELECTOR [*looking at him*]: What did you say? See how this harvest has increased our fame and glory. This flag here belongs to the Swedish body guard, does it not? [*He picks up a flag, unfurls it, and contemplates it.*]

KOTTWITZ: Your Majesty?

FIELD MARSHAL: My Lord?

ELECTOR: Yes, indeed! and from King Gustave Adolf's time. What does the inscription say?

KOTTWITZ: I believe . . .

FIELD MARSHAL: Per aspera ad astra.

ELECTOR: These words did not prove true at Fehrbellin.

[*Pause.*]

KOTTWITZ [*shyly*]: Your Majesty, grant me a word.

ELECTOR: What is it? Take everything . . . the flags, drums, and standards and hang them on the columns of the church. I plan to use them tomorrow for the victory celebration.

[*The Elector turns to the couriers, takes their dispatches, breaks open the seals, and reads them.*]

KOTTWITZ [*to himself*]: By the living God, he's pushing this a little too far.

[*Kottwitz, after some hesitation, picks up his two flags; the other officers and troops follow suit. At last, since the Prince's three flags remain on the floor, Kottwitz picks them up as well so that he now carries five.*]

OFFICER [*stepping before the Prince*]: Prince, your sword, please.

HOHENZOLLERN [*with his flag, stepping to the Prince's side*]: Stay calm, my friend!

PRINCE: Am I dreaming? Am I awake? Do I live? Am I in my right mind?

GOLTZ: Prince, I advise you to hand over your sword and say nothing.

PRINCE: I, a prisoner?

HOHENZOLLERN: Yes, you are.

GOLTZ: You heard him.

PRINCE: May one know why?

HOHENZOLLERN [*with emphasis*]: Not now. As we told you from the start, you plunged into battle prematurely. The order was not to move from the spot until commanded.

PRINCE: Help me, my friends, help! I'm going mad.

GOLTZ [*interrupting*]: Be quiet, don't say a word!

PRINCE: Have our troops been beaten, then?

HOHENZOLLERN [*stamping his foot*]: That's beside the point. The law must be obeyed.

PRINCE [*bitterly*]: So! That's it. So, so!

HOHENZOLLERN [*leaving him*]: It won't cost you your life.

GOLTZ [*likewise*]: Perhaps you'll have your freedom by tomorrow.

[*The Elector folds the letters together and returns to the circle of officers.*]

PRINCE [*after unbuckling his sword*]: My cousin Friedrich wants to play the role of Brutus and already sees himself seated on the Roman throne as in a painting: the Swedish flags are in the foreground and on the table the Brandenburg articles of war. By God, he shall not find in me the son who will admire him from underneath the executioner's ax. I have a German heart of the old-fashioned kind which is used to generosity and love. If he can now approach me only like a rigid figure from antiquity, I am sorry for him and he has earned my pity. [*He gives his sword to the officer and leaves.*]

ELECTOR: Bring him to headquarters at Fehrbellin, and there convene the court-martial that will judge him.

[*The Elector goes into the church followed by officers with their flags. The flags are then placed on columns while the Elector, together with his retinue, kneels in prayer at the side of Froben's coffin. Funeral music is heard.*]

CURTAIN

Act III

SCENE 1

Scene: Fehrbellin. A prison.

[*The Prince of Homburg. In the rear, two cavalrymen stand guard. Count Hohenzollern enters.*]

PRINCE: Ah, it's you, Heinrich. I'm glad to see you, my friend. Well, have I been released at last?

HOHENZOLLERN [*astonished*]: Oh, for heaven's sake!

PRINCE: What did you say?

HOHENZOLLERN: Released? Has he returned your sword to you?

PRINCE: To me? No!

HOHENZOLLERN: He hasn't?

PRINCE: No!

HOHENZOLLERN: Then what makes you think you're free?

PRINCE [*after a pause*]: I thought that you . . . that you were bringing me my freedom. Well, it doesn't matter!

HOHENZOLLERN: I have no news.

PRINCE: It doesn't matter, don't you hear? It doesn't matter! He'll send someone else to tell me. [*He turns around and brings some chairs.*] Have a seat! Come, now, tell me what's new. Has the Elector returned from Berlin?

HOHENZOLLERN [*distracted*]: Yes, yesterday evening.

PRINCE: Did the victory celebration take place there as planned? But, of course, it did! Was the Elector present in the church?

HOHENZOLLERN: Yes, with the Electress and Natalia. The church was illuminated with appropriate dignity and through-out the service of thanksgiving one could hear the cannon from the castle square resound in solemn splendor. The Swedish flags and standards fluttered like trophies on all the church's pillars. And, at the Elector's express command, your name was mentioned from the pulpit as the victorious hero of the battle.

PRINCE: So I've heard. Well, what else is new? What other news have you brought? Your expression, my friend, does not seem very cheerful.

HOHENZOLLERN: Have you spoken to anyone else yet?

PRINCE: To Goltz, just now . . . at the castle where I was being questioned, as you know.

[*Pause.*]

HOHENZOLLERN [*looking at him with misgivings*]: Well, Ar-thur, how do *you* view your situation since it has taken such an unexpected turn?

PRINCE: How do I view it? I think as you and Goltz do . . . and as the judges do too. The Elector has fulfilled his duty as required by the law. Now he will also listen to the promptings of his heart. "You've been at fault," he'll tell me in a solemn voice, and perhaps he'll add a word or too concerning death and prison: "Nevertheless, I will give you back your freedom." And around the sword with which I gave *him* victory, perhaps he'll wind some token of his favor. And, if not, that's all right too, since I really don't deserve it!

HOHENZOLLERN: Oh, Arthur! [*He stops short.*]

PRINCE: Well, what?

HOHENZOLLERN: Are you so sure of him?

PRINCE: This is how I see it! I mean a lot to him, that much I know. He loves me like a son and has proved it in a thousand ways ever since my earliest childhood. What doubts could possibly be troubling you? Didn't he seem to be even more pleased than I myself each time my fame grew greater? Has he not made me everything I am? Could he . . . could he really now be so devoid of love that he would trample into dust the plant which he himself has nurtured, just because it flowered a little too soon and with too much show? His worst enemy could not make me credit him with such behavior. So much less can you, who know and love him.

HOHENZOLLERN [*with emphasis*]: Arthur! You can still believe all this after having stood before the military court?

PRINCE: Yes! Because I stood before it. No one goes so far who does not intend to grant a pardon. It was precisely there, before the bar of justice, that I regained my confidence. After all, was it really a capital crime to have routed the Swedish army two minutes before the order came? And what other offense could I possibly be guilty of? How could he have summoned me before those heartless judges who sat like owls and hooted at me a constant funeral song of bullets—how could he have done this unless he thought of finally appearing like a God within their circle, there to utter his serene majestic pardon? No, my friend! He is gathering this night of clouds around my head only so that he can rise through the mists in radiance before me like the sun. And, quite frankly, I don't begrudge him this caprice.

HOHENZOLLERN: All the same, they say your sentence has been passed.

PRINCE: Yes, so I've heard . . . the death sentence.

HOHENZOLLERN [*astonished*]: You know it already?

PRINCE: Goltz, who was present at the sentencing, reported the court's verdict to me.

HOHENZOLLERN: Well, then, for God's sake—this fact does not upset you?

PRINCE: Upset me? Not in the least.

HOHENZOLLERN: You madman! On what do you base this certainty of yours?

PRINCE: On a feeling I have about him! [*He stands up.*] Leave me alone, I beg you! Why should I torture myself with useless doubts? [*He reflects a moment and sits down again. Pause.*] The court was forced to sentence me to death; so the law demands by which it acts. But before he'd sacrifice this loyal and loving heart to a bullet, before he'd end my life with a mere wave of a scarf . . . he'd sooner . . . can't you see that? . . . he'd sooner bare his own chest and pour his own blood drop by drop into the dust.

HOHENZOLLERN: But, Arthur, I assure you . . .

PRINCE [*impatiently*]: Oh, not again!

HOHENZOLLERN: The Field Marshal . . .

PRINCE [*as before*]: Let me be, my friend!

HOHENZOLLERN: Listen, I just have one more thing to say. And if this also means nothing to you, I'll say no more.

PRINCE [*turning his back on him*]: But I've told you, I know everything. Oh, well, what is it?

HOHENZOLLERN: The Field Marshal . . . and this is most peculiar . . . has just sent the death sentence to the castle. And the Elector, far from exercising his prerogative to pardon, has ordered that it be sent to him for signing.

PRINCE: It doesn't matter, I'm telling you.

HOHENZOLLERN: It doesn't matter?

PRINCE: For signing, did you say?

HOHENZOLLERN: Upon my word of honor! I can assure you of it.

PRINCE: The death sentence? No! The written verdict . . . ?

HOHENZOLLERN: It was the death sentence.

PRINCE: Who told you that?

HOHENZOLLERN: The Field Marshal himself.

PRINCE: When?

HOHENZOLLERN: Just now.

PRINCE: After he came back from seeing the Elector?

HOHENZOLLERN: As he was coming down the castle steps. He added . . . since he saw me so distraught . . . that all was not yet lost. Tomorrow brings another day on which you could be pardoned. But his white lips contradicted the words they spoke and revealed the fear that this would never happen!

PRINCE [*standing up*]: He couldn't possibly harbor such a monstrous decision in his heart, could he? He couldn't possibly trample into dust the giver of a diamond just because the diamond had a tiny flaw scarcely visible even through a magnifying glass. An act like this would turn the blackness of the warlord of Algiers white. It would decorate the pleasure-loving Sardanapalus with cherubic wings of shimmering silver. It would place at God's right hand the entire line of ancient Roman tyrants and make them guiltless . . . like infants who have died upon their mothers' breasts.

HOHENZOLLERN [*who has also risen*]: My friend, try to recognize your situation!

PRINCE: And the Field Marshal kept silent and said nothing?

51

HOHENZOLLERN: What was there to say?

PRINCE: Oh, God! All my hopes are gone!

HOHENZOLLERN: Have you ever done anything . . . to your knowledge or unconsciously . . . that might have seemed to challenge his proud will?

PRINCE: Never!

HOHENZOLLERN: Think carefully!

PRINCE: Never. I swear it! The very shadow of his head was sacred to me.

HOHENZOLLERN: Arthur, now don't be angry with me if I doubt your words. Count Horn, the Swedish envoy, has arrived, and his business, so I've been assured, concerns the Princess of Orange. But something that your aunt, the Electress, let slip has offended the Elector most profoundly. It is said that the Princess has already given her heart to someone else. Are you not involved here in some way?

PRINCE: Oh, God! What are you telling me?

HOHENZOLLERN: Are you the one? Are you?

PRINCE: Yes, my friend, I am. Now everything is clear to me. My understanding with the Princess plunges me in ruin! Know, then, that I am to blame for her refusal. She has promised her hand to me.

HOHENZOLLERN: You reckless fool! What have you done? How many times have I not warned you as a loyal friend?

PRINCE: Oh, my friend! Help me! Save me! I am lost!

HOHENZOLLERN: Of course, I will, but where's the way out from this desperate situation? Perhaps you would like to speak with your aunt, the Electress?

PRINCE [*turning around*]: Hey, guard!

CAVALRY SOLDIER [*in the background*]: Here!

PRINCE: Call your officer! [*He quickly takes a coat from the wall and puts on a plumed hat which is lying on the table.*]

HOHENZOLLERN [*helping him*]: This move, if shrewdly carried out, could save your life. For if the Elector can only conclude a peace treaty with King Karl . . . at that special price of which we're both aware . . . then you'll see, his heart will once again be reconciled to you and you will have your freedom right away . . . within a few short hours.

SCENE 2

[*The Officer enters. The others remain*]

PRINCE [*to the officer*]: Strantz, I am in your custody. Permit me to leave this prison for one hour on an urgent matter.

OFFICER: Prince, you have not been remanded into my custody. According to my orders, you are free to go wherever you wish.

PRINCE: That's strange! Then I'm not a prisoner?

OFFICER: Forgive me for saying so, but your word is bond enough.

PRINCE [*setting off*]: I see. It doesn't matter. Very well, then. So, goodbye.

HOHENZOLLERN: The Prince will drag his chains along with him wherever he goes.

PRINCE: I'm only going to the castle to see my aunt, and will be back again very shortly.

[*They all leave.*]

SCENE 3

Scene: the Electress's rooms.

[*The Electress and Princess Natalia enter.*]

ELECTRESS: Come along, my dear, do come! Now is your chance. Count Gustave Horn, the Swedish envoy, and his delegation have left the castle, and I see a light in your uncle's chamber. Come, now, put on your shawl and tiptoe in to him. Try to see if you can save your friend.

[*They are about to leave.*]

SCENE 4

[*Enter a lady-in-waiting. The others remain.*]

LADY-IN-WAITING: Madam, the Prince of Homburg is waiting at the door. I could scarcely believe my eyes!

ELECTRESS [*taken aback*]: Oh, my God!

NATALIA: The Prince himself?

ELECTRESS: Isn't he under arrest?

LADY-IN-WAITING: He is standing outside the door in his cloak and feathered hat and appears to be extremely upset. He implores you for an audience and says it's urgent.

ELECTRESS [*annoyed*]: The reckless fool, to break his word in such a manner!

NATALIA: Who knows what's driven him here?

ELECTRESS [*upon reflection*]: Let him enter. [*She sits down in a chair.*]

SCENE 5

[*The Prince of Homburg enters. The others remain.*]

PRINCE: Mother! [*He falls on his knees before her.*]

ELECTRESS: Prince! What are you doing here?

PRINCE: I am here to beg for mercy, mother!

ELECTRESS [*with suppressed emotion*]: You are a prisoner, Prince, how is it that you are here? Why are you adding new guilt to the old?

PRINCE [*urgently*]: Do you know what has happened to me?

ELECTRESS: I know everything. But what can I, a helpless woman, do for you?

PRINCE: Oh, mother! You would not speak like that if death were creeping toward you as it is toward me. You seem to me endowed with powers of Heaven, with the power to save . . . and so does Princess Natalia, so do your ladies here, and everyone around me. I could fling my arms about the neck of your stableboy, the lowest servant in your house who does nothing more than care for horses, and plead with *him* to save me. Of all God's creatures here on earth, I alone am helpless; only I have been abandoned and can do nothing, nothing at all!

ELECTRESS: You are quite beside yourself. What has happened?

PRINCE: Oh, God! As I was walking down the path that led

me here, I saw the grave that is to hold my bones tomorrow; in the light shed by the torches, I saw it open up before me! They want to draw the shades of night across these eyes, dear aunt, with which I see you now; they want to pierce this chest with deadly bullets. On the market square, even the windows have already been reserved that will look down upon the desolate spectacle of my execution. And he, who standing on life's summit now, can still look out upon the future as if upon a wondrous realm . . . that man will lie between two narrow boards tomorrow, stinking. And only a stone will remain to tell you: he once was!

[*The Princess, who until now has been standing in the background, leaning on the shoulder of a lady-in-waiting, is greatly shaken by these words and sits down at a table, weeping.*]

ELECTRESS: My son! If this be God's will, you must arm yourself with courage and with self-control!

PRINCE: But God's world is so beautiful, mother! I beg you, do not let me go down into the shadows of darkness before my time has come! Let him punish me in some other way, if I have been in error. Why does it have to be with bullets? Let him take away my offices, let him cashier me, if the law demands it, and discharge me from the army with dishonor. God in heaven! Since I have seen my grave, I only want to live, and care no more for honor!

ELECTRESS: Stand up, my son, stand up! What are you saying? You are going to pieces! Pull yourself together!

PRINCE: No, aunt, not until you promise me that you will approach your exalted husband on your knees to save my life, not until you promise to plead with him on my behalf. Hedwig, your childhood friend, gave me into your keeping when she lay dying in Homburg. She said: "You be his mother when I am gone." Deeply moved, you knelt down beside her bed and, bending over her, you gave your pledge: "He shall be as dear to me as if I myself had borne him." Well, I now remind you of those words! Go, then, as if you really were the one who'd borne me, and say: "I beg for mercy, for mercy! Let him go!" Yes, and come back to me and say: "You are free!"

ELECTRESS [*weeping*]: My dear son! I have already done that! But all my pleading was in vain!

PRINCE: I give up every claim to happiness. Natalia's hand in marriage . . . and don't forget to tell him this . . . I don't want it any more. All affection that I ever felt for her has died within my heart. She is once again as free as a deer on the heath, free to give her hand and heart to anyone she wants, as if I had never existed. And even should she give herself to Karl Gustave, the King of Sweden, I would praise her choice. I only want to go back to my estates along the Rhine. There I will build, tear down, and build again until I drip with sweat; there, although I am alone, I will sow and reap as if for wife and child. And after I have reaped my harvest, I will plough once more and so chase life around a circle until it sinks as evening falls . . . and dies!

ELECTRESS: Very well! But now return to your prison. That is the first condition of my favor.

PRINCE [*He stands up and turns to the Princess.*]: Poor girl, you are crying! Today the sun is lighting the path that leads all your hopes into their grave. I know that your first feelings of love were for me, and the expression on your face now tells me, clear as day, that you will never devote yourself to another man. But what can I, the poorest of men, give you that would be of comfort to you now? My advice is that you go to your cousin Thurn, to live inside her nunnery on the River Main. Find yourself a little boy in the mountains, whose hair is curly blond like mine. Buy him for yourself with gold and silver, press him to your heart, and teach him how to stammer out the word: "Mother"! And when he grows older, show him how to close the eyes of dying men. That is all the happiness that is in store for you!

NATALIA [*Encouraged and inspired, she stands up and places her hand in that of the Prince.*]: Return, young hero, to the custody of your prison. And on your way back, take a second look, this time a calm look, at the grave that has been dug for you! It is in no way darker and by no means deeper than the grave which already has appeared to you a thousand times upon the field of battle. I will be faithful to you until death. In the meanwhile, I'll dare to speak to my uncle in the hope of saving you. Perhaps I will succeed in touching his heart, and so free you from all your sorrow!

[*Pause.*]

PRINCE [*Lost in rapturous contemplation of her, he folds his hands.*]: If you had two wings upon your shoulders, Natalia, I would truly take you for an angel. Oh, God! Did I really hear you say you'd speak for me? Where have you kept hidden till today the quiver of your speech's arrows . . . that you will dare to approach His Highness? Oh, a ray of hope now all at once revives me!

NATALIA: God himself will hand to me the arrows which will strike home. But if the Elector is unable to change the verdict of the law, is *unable to,* I say: so be it! Then you, brave hero, shall accept the law and submit to it with courage. The man who's won a thousand victories in life will know how to conquer death as well!

ELECTRESS: But go now! Valuable time, which we could use to help you, is flying by!

PRINCE: Well, may all the saints protect you! Farewell! Farewell! And whatever it is you may succeed in doing, send me a sign, some word of your success.

[*They all leave.*]

CURTAIN

Act IV

SCENE 1

Scene: The Elector's rooms.

[*The Elector, with papers in his hand, is standing near a table illuminated by candlelight. Natalia enters through a center door and kneels at some distance from him. Pause.*]

NATALIA [*kneeling*]: My noble uncle, Friedrich of Brandenburg.

ELECTOR [*putting the papers aside*]: Natalia! [*He goes to raise her up.*]

NATALIA: Let me be!

ELECTOR: What do you want, my dear?

NATALIA: To beg for mercy for my cousin Homburg, to plead here at your feet as is only fitting. I do not want to save him for myself! Although I have to tell you that I love him, I do not wish to save him for myself. Let him marry any woman he chooses. I only want to know that he's alive, alive and free and independent . . . like a flower that delights me. This I beg of you, my most sovereign Lord and friend. I know that you will listen to my prayer.

ELECTOR [*raising her*]: How can you ask such a thing, my little daughter! Do you not know what crime your cousin Homburg has committed?

NATALIA: Oh, dear uncle!

ELECTOR: Well? Did he or did he not commit a crime?

NATALIA: Oh, it was a little error . . . innocent as his blond hair and blue eyes. You should have raised him from the ground before he had a chance to beg for mercy. Surely, you will not destroy him and cast him from your side. No, you will press him to your heart for his dear mother's sake, and you will say: "Come, do not weep! You mean as much to me as loyalty itself!" Was it not his eagerness to glorify your name which seduced him into breaking through the limits set by law? And, oh, having broken the law with youthful folly, did he not then crush the dragon like a man in the heat of battle? First to place a crown upon his head because he was the victor in the battle and then to take his head away . . . surely, history does not require such a gesture from you. That would be so exalted, dear uncle, that one could almost call it an inhuman act. And yet, God has never created a gentler man than you.

ELECTOR: My sweet child! Look ; . . . if I were a tyrant, your words, and this I feel most strongly, would have already melted my heart of iron. Because I'm not, however, there's a question I must put to you: may I arbitrarily suppress the judgment handed down by my own court? What would be the consequences of such an action?

NATALIA: Consequences? For whom? For you?

ELECTOR: For me? No! Of course not for me! Don't you recognize anything higher than me, dear girl? Are you unacquainted with that holy thing that's known in army camps as fatherland?

NATALIA: Oh, my Lord! What are you worrying about? Our fatherland? Surely, Brandenburg will not disintegrate, our fatherland will not be shattered into ruins at this, the slightest gesture of your mercy. On the contrary, what you, who have been raised in army camps call disorder . . . and by this I mean your decision to rescind the court-martial's verdict in this particular case . . . such an act I'd term the very highest order. I know the laws of war should rule; however, the gentler feelings must also have their say. The fatherland which you, my dear uncle, have founded for our people stands solid like a fortress: it will yet withstand quite different storms than the Prince's capricious victory. And our fatherland will grow in size and beauty. In the hands of your grandchildren, it will stand resplendent with battlements and towers; it will stand luxuriant like a land in fairy tales . . . a joy to friends and a terror to our enemies. Our country does not need a cold and desolate law, nourished by a dear friend's blood, for it to live on past the autumn of my uncle's life, my splendid, peaceful uncle's reign.

ELECTOR: Does your cousin Homburg think as you do?

NATALIA: Cousin Homburg?

ELECTOR: Does he think it's all the same to the fatherland if impulse or if law prevails?

NATALIA: Oh, that boy!

ELECTOR: Well, does he?

NATALIA: Oh, dear uncle, tears are my only answer to this question.

ELECTOR [*taken aback*]: Why, my daughter? What has happened?

NATALIA [*hesitant*]: He now thinks of nothing but of rescue. The barrels of the firing squad's guns stare at him with such awe-inspiring horror that, confused and shocked as he is, they silence every other wish in him but the wish to live. He could see our whole Brandenburg sink amid lightning and thunder, beneath a raging storm, and not ask what's happening. My God, what a heroic heart it is you've crushed. [*She turns away and weeps.*]

ELECTOR [*extremely surprised*]: No, my dearest Natalia, it can't be possible! Is it true, he really begs for mercy?

NATALIA: Oh, if only you had never condemned him!

ELECTOR: No, tell me: does he beg for mercy? What has happened, my dear child? Why are you crying? You spoke with him? Tell me everything! You spoke with him?

NATALIA [*leaning against him*]: Yes, just now in the apartments of my aunt where he came furtively creeping under the cover of darkness, distraught and timid, a pitiable, wretched sight in his plumed hat and cloak. I would never have believed that a man whom history has proclaimed a hero could sink so low. I am a woman, and a mere worm that comes too close to my shoe frightens me away. And yet death, even if it appeared before me in a lion's hideous form, would not find me so completely crushed, so utterly devoid of self-control, so absolutely unheroic. Oh, what, indeed, is human greatness, human glory!

ELECTOR [*confused*]: Well, then, by heaven and earth, take heart, my child, he's free!

NATALIA: What, my noble Lord?

ELECTOR: He's pardoned. I'll draft the necessary release papers immediately.

NATALIA: Oh, my dearest friend. Is it really true?

ELECTOR: You have heard me.

NATALIA: He'll be pardoned? He won't have to die?

ELECTOR: My word of honor, I swear it to you. How could I dare to set myself in opposition to the convictions of such a warrior? You know that in my innermost self I have the highest regard for the Prince's feelings. If he can tell me that the verdict is unjust, I will set it aside and he'll be free. [*He brings Natalia a chair.*] Will you wait here for a moment? [*He goes to the table, sits down, and writes. Pause.*]

NATALIA [*to herself*]: Oh, my heart, why are you beating so furiously within your house?

ELECTOR [*writing*]: Is the Prince still at the castle?

NATALIA: No! He has returned to prison.

ELECTOR [*He finishes his letter and seals it. He then returns to Natalia with it.*]: Alas, my little daughter, my lovely niece has shed tears! And I, who was entrusted with her happiness, had to be the one who brought clouds to the gentle heavens of her eyes. [*He puts his arm around her.*] Would you like to bring the letter to him yourself?

NATALIA: To the prison? Really?

ELECTOR [*He presses the letter into her hands.*]: Why not? Hey, guards!

[*Castle guards in Hungarian dress enter.*]

Have the carriage brought. The Princess has business to transact with Colonel Homburg.

[*The guards leave.*]

If you take the letter to him now, he'll be able to thank you right away for his life. [*He embraces her.*] My dear child, are we friends again?

NATALIA [*after a pause*]: Whatever it was that so suddenly aroused your good will, my Lord, I do not know and do not wish to fathom. But I do know in my heart that you would not ignobly mock my feelings. The letter, however it may be phrased, contains, I think, the Prince's rescue . . . and for this I thank you. [*She kisses his hand.*]

ELECTOR: It does indeed, my little daughter, it certainly does. As surely as his rescue now depends on Cousin Homburg's wishes!

[*They leave.*]

SCENE 2

Scene: Apartments of the Princess.

[*Enter Princess Natalia followed by two ladies-in-waiting and Cavalry Captain Count Reuss.*]

NATALIA [*in haste*]: What do you have for me, Count? Is it from my regiment? Is it important? Can it wait until to-morrow?

REUSS [*handing her a letter*]: A letter from Colonel Kottwitz, Madam!

NATALIA: Quick, give it to me. What does it say? [*She opens it.*]

REUSS: It's a petition for His Majesty, our leader, on behalf of the Prince of Homburg, candid, yet respectful, as you can see.

NATALIA [*reads*]: "Petition from the Regiment of the Prin-cess of Orange, respectfully submitted."

[*Pause.*]

May I ask who drew up this petition?

REUSS: Probably Colonel Kottwitz himself, if one can guess from the awkward handwriting. Besides, it is his noble name that heads the list.

NATALIA: And the thirty signatures that follow his?

REUSS: Those, Madam, are the names of the other officers ac-cording to their rank.

NATALIA: But why has the petition been forwarded to me?

REUSS: Because, Madam, we wish to ask you in all humility whether you, as chief of our regiment, wish to enter your name on the first line which has been left free.

[*Pause.*]

NATALIA: I hear that such a step is no longer necessary since the Prince, my noble cousin, is to be pardoned by His Majesty upon his own initiative.

REUSS [*pleased*]: What? Really?

NATALIA: Nevertheless, I shall not refuse you. I shall sign at the top as you wish and thus place myself in the forefront of this endeavor. Who knows but that such a document, cleverly handled, could tip the scales in His Majesty's consideration of this matter. Perhaps he'll even welcome it in making his decision. [*She goes to sign her name.*]

REUSS: We'll be greatly in your debt.

[*Pause.*]

NATALIA [*turning to Reuss again*]: But, Count Reuss, I only see my regiment on the list. Why don't I see the names of the Bomsdorf cuirassiers and the dragoons from Götz and Anhalt-Pless?

REUSS: Not, as you may fear, because their hearts beat more timidly than ours. Unfortunately for our plan, Kottwitz was stationed far away in Arnstein. Thus he was separated from the regiments whose camps lie right here near the city. There was no safe and easy way to send the petition round to all those regiments.

NATALIA: All the same, without those other names I fear your petition lacks sufficient weight. Are you certain, Count, that if you had also been stationed here and could have spoken with the other troops that they would have joined with you and given their support?

REUSS: The troops stationed here, Madam? To the last man! The entire cavalry has pledged itself to our cause. I believe the entire army of Brandenburg would have inscribed their names.

NATALIA [*after a pause*]: Then why don't you dispatch officers to the camps to hand round the petition?

REUSS: Forgive me! Colonel Kottwitz would not approve. He said he did not wish to take any action which could be misconstrued.

NATALIA: What a strange old man he is! First he's bold and then he's timid. Fortunately, I've just remembered that His Majesty, who is hard pressed by other matters, has commissioned me to send orders to Kottwitz to here with his troops, since the stables in Arnstein are inadequate. I must sit down and write the orders now. [*She sits down and writes.*]

REUSS: It's perfect, Madam! No turn of events could be more favorable to our petition.

NATALIA [*while writing*]: Then use it to advantage, Count Reuss! [*She finishes writing, seals the document, and rises.*] Understand, however, that these orders are to remain in your dispatch case for the moment. Do not leave for Arnstein and hand them over to Colonel Kottwitz until I have given you more definite instructions.

[*She gives him the orders. A castle guard in Hungarian dress enters.*]

GUARD: Madam, the carriage His Majesty ordered is waiting in the courtyard.

NATALIA: Bring it to the door. I'll be down directly. [*Pause, in which she approaches the table deep in thought and puts on her gloves.*] Count, would you care to accompany me to the Prince of Homburg, with whom I wish to speak? There is room for you in my carriage.

REUSS: Madam, this honor, indeed . . . ! [*He offers her his arm.*]

NATALIA [*to the ladies-in-waiting*]: Dear friends, follow me. Perhaps I shall decide about Colonel Kottwitz's orders over there.

SCENE 3

Scene: The Prince's cell.

[*The Prince of Homburg hangs his hat on the wall and sits down despondently on cushions spread out on the floor.*]

PRINCE: Life, as a dervish once said, is a journey and a short one at that. First we rise six feet above the earth and then lie six feet under. But I now want to settle down somewhere in between. Today a man can carry his head proudly upon his shoulders. By tomorrow it may tremble on his neck and lie the next day at his feet. They say, of course, the sun also shines in the next world and upon brighter fields than ours. It's only a pity that the eye must rot before it can see such splendors.

SCENE 4

[*Enter, Princess Natalia accompanied by Cavalry Captain Reuss and followed by ladies-in-waiting. A courier with a torch precedes them. The Prince.*]

COURIER: Her Highness, the Princess of Orange.

PRINCE [*rising*]: Natalia!

COURIER: Here she comes.

NATALIA [*bowing to Reuss*]: Kindly leave us for a few moments.

[*Reuss and the courier leave.*]

PRINCE: My dearest lady.

NATALIA: Dear, good cousin.

PRINCE [*leading her forward*]: Tell me, what news do you bring? Speak, how do matters stand?

NATALIA: Well, everything's all right. As I predicted, you've been pardoned; you are free. Here is a letter from his hand which will confirm what I've said.

PRINCE: It can't be possible. No! It's a dream.

NATALIA: Read! Read the letter and see for yourself!

PRINCE [*reading*]: "My Prince of Homburg. When I placed you under arrest because of your all too premature attack, I believed that I was only doing my duty, and I counted upon your approval. But if you believe that I have treated you unjustly, I beg you to let me know with two words, and I will return your sword to you immediately."

[*Natalia turns pale. Pause. The Prince looks at her questioningly.*]

NATALIA [*with an expression of sudden joy*]: Well, then, there it is. Only two words are necessary. My dear, sweet friend! [*She presses his hand.*]

PRINCE: My dear Lady!

NATALIA: Oh, what a blissful hour has finally dawned! Here, take the pen, take it and write him!

PRINCE: And this is his signature?

NATALIA: Yes, the letter "F." It's his initial. Oh, Lady Bork!

Oh, please, everyone be happy. His generosity is boundless as the sea, I knew it! Bring the Prince a chair! He should compose his answer right away.

PRINCE: He says, if I believe . . . ?

NATALIA [*interrupting him*]: Of course! Hurry up! Sit down! I want to dictate the letter to you. [*She places a chair behind him.*]

PRINCE: I want to read the letter once again.

NATALIA [*tearing the letter out of his hand*]: What for? Haven't you already seen your grave in the churchyard yawning toward you with open jaws? The matter is urgent. Sit down and write!

PRINCE [*smiling*]: Really, you're acting as if the grave were about to pounce on me like a panther. [*He sits down and picks up his pen.*]

NATALIA [*She turns away and weeps.*]: If you do not wish to make me angry, please write the letter now.

[*The Prince rings for a servant. The servant enters.*]

PRINCE: Paper and pen, seal and wax.

[*The servant, having brought these things, leaves again. The Prince writes. Pause.*]

PRINCE [*He tears up the letter he has begun and throws it under the table*]: A stupid beginning! [*He takes another sheet of paper.*]

NATALIA [*picking up the letter*]: What? What did you say? My God, it's very good; why, it's excellent!

PRINCE [*muttering*]: Worthy of a scoundrel not a prince. I must think of another turn of phrase. [*Pause. He reaches for the Elector's letter, which the Princess is holding in her hand.*] What is it the letter says?

NATALIA [*refusing to give him the letter*]: Nothing, nothing at all.

PRINCE: Give it to me.

NATALIA: But you've read it already.

PRINCE [*seizing it*]: So what? I only want to see how I should phrase my answer. [*He unfolds the letter and rereads it.*]

NATALIA [*to herself*]: Oh, God of the world! He's done for.

PRINCE [*stunned*]: Look, here! His letter is exceedingly strange. You probably overlooked this sentence!

NATALIA: No, I didn't. Which sentence?

PRINCE: He calls upon me to make the decision myself.

NATALIA: So he does.

PRINCE: Very upright, indeed, very dignified. He's conducted himself as a person must who has a noble heart.

NATALIA: Oh, my friend, his generosity is without bounds. Now you must do your part and write as he deserves. You see, your answer serves only as the pretext to satisfy an external formality. As soon as he has your words in hand, the whole difficulty is at an end.

PRINCE [*putting the letter aside*]: No, my love. I want to consider the matter until tomorrow.

NATALIA: I don't understand you at all. What a turnabout? Why? What for?

PRINCE [*Filled with passion, he gets up from the chair.*]: I beg you, do not ask me! You have not weighed carefully the contents of the letter. I cannot fulfill the condition he has set me and write him that he treated me unfairly. If you force me to respond now, in my present mood, then, by God, I'll write him that he's treated me with perfect justice. [*He sits down and, leaning on the table with his arms folded, he contemplates the letter.*]

NATALIA [*pale*]: You madman! What are you saying? [*Deeply moved, she bends over him.*]

PRINCE [*pressing her hand*]: Wait a minute! It seems to me . . . [*He reflects.*]

NATALIA: What did you say?

PRINCE: I think I shall soon know what I have to write.

NATALIA [*in anguish*]: Homburg!

PRINCE [*taking up the pen*]: I'm listening . . . what is it?

NATALIA: My dear friend! I admire the impulse that has taken hold of you. But I swear to you that the regiment has already been ordered, and it is resigned to carry out your death sentence tomorrow. As you stand upon the mound beside your grave, they will fire their muskets and you will disappear from the face of the earth. If you are too noble to deny the verdict of the court, too honorable to contradict it as his letter here demands . . . well, then, I can assure you that he'll act sublimely and, as matters stand, will have your death sentence carried out completely devoid of mercy.

PRINCE [*writing*]: It doesn't matter.

NATALIA: It doesn't matter?

PRINCE: He is free to act as he pleases; now I must act as befits a prince.

NATALIA [*She approaches the Prince in shock.*]: You monster! I believe you've already composed your answer.

PRINCE [*He finishes writing the letter*]: "Homburg. Fehrbellin. Dated the twelfth . . ." Yes, I'm finished. Franz! [*He places the letter in an envelope and seals it.*]

NATALIA: Oh, God in heaven!

PRINCE [*rising*]: Take this letter to the castle and hand it to His Majesty.

[*The servant leaves.*]

PRINCE: I can't act in an ignoble fashion toward a man who has treated me with such nobility. Guilt, grave guilt lies heavily upon me, and I now recognize it. If his forgiveness must depend upon my arguing the issue with him, then I don't want his pardon.

NATALIA [*kissing him*]: Take this kiss! And if twelve bullets now dashed you to the ground, I would have to rejoice even as I wept and tell you I approved. However, since you feel free to follow the promptings of your heart, I must be allowed to follow mine as well. Count Reuss!

[*The courier opens the door. The Count enters.*]

REUSS: Here I am.

NATALIA: Leave for Arnstein with your letter to Colonel Kottwitz. His Majesty commands the regiment to march, and I shall expect it here before midnight.

[*They all leave.*]

CURTAIN

Act V

SCENE 1

Scene: Room in the castle.

[*The Elector, partially dressed, enters from an adjoining room followed by Count Truchss, Count Hohenzollern, and Cavalry Captain von der Goltz. Pages with torches.*]

ELECTOR: Kottwitz? With the Princess's dragoons? Here in the city?

TRUCHSS [*opening the window*]: Yes, Your Majesty. He's marched them here, and they're gathered in front of the castle now.

ELECTOR: Well, gentlemen, does anyone want to solve this riddle for me? Who summoned Kottwitz here?

HOHENZOLLERN: That I do not know, my Sovereign.

ELECTOR: I assigned him to a place called Arnstein. Quickly, one of you, go and bring him here.

GOLTZ: My Lord, he will appear before you immediately.

ELECTOR: Where is he now?

GOLTZ: I hear he's at the City Hall, where your entire general staff is meeting.

ELECTOR: What for? To what end?

HOHENZOLLERN: That I don't know.

TRUCHSS: My Prince and Lord, will you grant us leave to go there too?

ELECTOR: Where? To the City Hall?

HOHENZOLLERN: To a meeting of the army's chiefs. We gave our word that we'd appear.

ELECTOR [*after a short pause*]: You are dismissed.

GOLTZ: Come, my friends.

[*The officers leave.*]

SCENE 2

[*The Elector. Later two servants.*]

ELECTOR: How strange! If I were the Dey of Tunis I would sound the alarm at such an ambiguous situation. I would place the silken noose upon my desk. I'd barricade the gates and bring out cannon. But since it's only Hans Kottwitz from Priegnitz who's taken it upon himself to approach me in this unauthorized fashion, I will conduct myself in Brandenburg style. I'll just take hold of one of the three shining silver locks on his trusty old head and quietly lead him with his twelve squadrons back to Arnstein. Why wake the whole city from its sleep?

[*After once again looking out of the window for a moment, he goes back to his table and rings. Two servants enter.*]

ELECTOR: Run down and find out what's going on in the City Hall. But pretend you're asking for yourself.

SERVANT: Immediately, Your Majesty.

[*One of the servants leaves.*]

ELECTOR [*to the other servant*]: You go and bring me my clothes.

[*The servant goes and brings them. The Elector dresses and puts on his official regalia.*]

SCENE 3

[*Enter Field Marshal Dörfling. The above.*]

FIELD MARSHAL: It's rebellion, Your Majesty!

ELECTOR [*busy dressing*]: Be still, be quiet! You know how much I hate being intruded upon in my chambers unannounced. What do you want?

FIELD MARSHAL: Sire, please forgive me, but an urgent matter has driven me here. Colonel Kottwitz has marched into the city without orders. A hundred officers have gathered round him in the Hall of Knights, and a petition has been circulated which is designed to interfere with your prerogatives.

ELECTOR: I know all about it already. What else can it be but an undertaking on behalf of the Prince, who has been condemned by the law to be shot.

FIELD MARSHAL: That's just it! You've guessed it exactly!

ELECTOR: Well, good. Then my heart is with them.

FIELD MARSHAL: I've heard that these madmen intend to hand you their petition this very day in the castle. And should you with unbending anger insist upon the sentence, then . . .

and I scarcely dare to tell you . . . they plan to liberate him from his prison by force.

ELECTOR [*gravely*]: Who told you that?

FIELD MARSHAL: Who told me that? Lady Retzow, my wife's cousin, whom you can trust. Last night she was at her uncle Bailiff Retzow's house where officers who had come from camp were talking about this audacious plan.

ELECTOR: I'll have to hear this from a man before I'll believe it. And . . . I myself will stand before the Prince's prison and protect him from these young heroes.

FIELD MARSHAL: Majesty, I beg you! If you have the slightest intention of pardoning the Prince, do it now before a most abominable act has been committed. Every army loves its hero, as you know. Do not let the spark which merely glimmers now among the men burst out into an all-devouring blaze which will destroy everything it touches. Neither Kottwitz nor the men who've gathered round him know that I have warned you. Before he arrives here return the Prince's sword to him, send it back as he in truth deserves. In this way, you'll give the newspapers one more deed of generosity to report and one act of cruelty less.

ELECTOR: I would have to ask the Prince first if I may do this, since, as you are aware, he was not arbitrarily imprisoned and so cannot arbitrarily be freed. I should like to speak with these gentlemen when they come.

FIELD MARSHAL [*to himself*]: Damn! He's armed against every weapon.

SCENE 4

[*Two castle guards dressed as Hungarian foot soldiers enter. One has a letter in his hand. The above.*]

FIRST GUARD: Colonel Kottwitz, Hennings, Truchss, and others request an audience.

ELECTOR [*to the other guard while taking the letter from him*]: From the Prince of Homburg?

SECOND GUARD: Yes, Your Majesty.

ELECTOR: Who gave it to you?

SECOND GUARD: The Swiss soldier who's keeping guard at the gate and who himself received it from the Prince's orderly.

ELECTOR [*He goes over to the table to read it. After finishing, he turns and calls a page.*]: Prittwitz! Bring me the death warrant! I also want the safe conduct pass for Count Gustave Horn, the Swedish envoy. [*As the page leaves, he turns to the first guard.*] Let Kottwitz and his entourage come in.

SCENE 5

[*Colonel Kottwitz and Colonel Hennings, Count Truchss, Count Hohenzollern, Count Sparren, Count Reuss, Cavalry Captains Goltz and Strantz, and other colonels and officers enter. The above.*]

KOTTWITZ [*with the petition*]: Allow me, Your Highness, to hand you this document in all humility and in the name of the entire army.

ELECTOR: Kottwitz, before I take it, tell me who ordered you to march into the city.

KOTTWITZ [*staring at him*]: With the dragoons?

ELECTOR: With the regiment. I designated Arnstein as your headquarters.

KOTTWITZ: Majesty, it was your orders that brought me here.

ELECTOR: What? Show them to me.

KOTTWITZ: Here, my Lord.

ELECTOR [*reading*]: "Natalia, signed at Fehrbellin, in the name of my most sovereign uncle Friedrich."

KOTTWITZ: By God, my Prince and Lord, I dare not imagine that these orders are unknown to you.

ELECTOR: Of course not, don't misunderstand me. But who is it who brought the orders to you?

KOTTWITZ: Count Reuss.

ELECTOR [*after a short pause*]: All the better; I welcome you here. You have been chosen with your twelve squadrons to perform the last honors tomorrow morning for the Prince of Homburg, whom the law has sentenced to death.

KOTTWITZ [*shocked*]: What, Your Majesty?

ELECTOR [*returning Kottwitz's orders*]: Is your regiment still standing out there in front of the castle in the darkness and the mist?

KOTTWITZ: In the darkness? I beg your pardon . . .

ELECTOR: Why didn't you quarter the men?

KOTTWITZ: My Lord, they have been quartered . . . right here in the city as you ordered.

ELECTOR [*turning to the window*]: What already? But just two minutes ago . . . Well, you've certainly found stables quickly enough. All the better. I welcome you once again! Tell me, what brings you here? What news do you have?

KOTTWITZ: Majesty, the petition of your loyal army.

ELECTOR: Give it to me.

KOTTWITZ: But the words you've just spoken have crushed all my hope.

ELECTOR: Then words can raise it up again. [*He reads.*] "Petition begging for mercy for our leader, the General Prince Friedrich Hessen-Homburg, who has been sentenced to death." [*To the officers*] A noble name, gentlemen, a name not unworthy of your support in such great number. [*He looks once again at the document.*] Who wrote the petition?

KOTTWITZ: I did.

ELECTOR: Is the Prince acquainted with its content?

KOTTWITZ: Not in the least. It was conceived and executed by us alone.

ELECTOR: A moment's patience, if you please. [*He steps up to the table and reads the petition. Long pause.*] Hm, very strange! You, an old warrior, defend the Prince's act and justify the fact that he attacked Wrangel without my orders?

KOTTWITZ: Yes, Your Majesty! Kottwitz does.

ELECTOR: On the battlefield you did not hold this view.

KOTTWITZ: My opinion then was ill considered, my Lord. I should have peacefully submitted to the Prince, who understands the art of war quite well. The Swedes were wavering on their left flank, but support was coming from the right. If at this point the Prince had stopped to wait for orders, they would have re-established outposts in the trenches and you would never have had your victory.

ELECTOR: So! That's the way you like to fantasize the outcome. However, as you know, I had dispatched Colonel Hennings to take the Swedish bridgehead which protected Wrangel's rear lines, and if you had not disobeyed my orders, Henning's mission would have been successful. Within two hours he would have been able to burn the enemy's bridges and position our own troops along the Rhyn. Wrangel would have been completely annihilated in the swamps and trenches.

KOTTWITZ: A man of mediocrity and not a man like you needs to feel he has to wrest from fate the greatest laurel wreaths of victory. Indeed, until today you always accepted whatever it was that fate had to give. The dragon who defiantly destroyed the state of Brandenburg has been driven off with a bleeding skull. What more could you have wanted in one day? What does it matter to you if he lies another two weeks exhausted in the sand and heals his wounds? What does matter is that we've learned how to defeat him and cannot wait to exercise our skill again. Just let us boldly meet with Wrangel face to face once more and our victory will be complete. Then the Swedes will have to flee into the Baltic. Rome, after all, was not built in a day.

ELECTOR: You fool, how can you expect a permanent victory when each and every one is permitted to grab the reigns of my war chariot and drive it as he wishes. Do you think that fortune will always reward disobedience with a crown of victory as it did at Fehrbellin? I do not want a victory that's a child of chance, a victory that falls into my lap like a bastard child. I must uphold the law, the mother of my crown, who will yet bear me a whole race of victories.

KOTTWITZ: Majesty, the highest law . . . the law that inspires the leaders of your army is not the letter of your will; it is the fatherland, it is the crown, it is you yourself upon whose head it rests. Why should you care according to what rules the enemy is beaten . . . if only it falls before you with its banners. The rule which defeats the foe is the best rule of all. Do you wish to transform the army which follows you with glowing passion into a mere instrument, like the sword which rests lifeless in your golden belt? It was an impoverished spirit who first proclaimed a precept such as this. Yes, statecraft is a poor, shortsighted thing indeed when it chooses to forget emotions merely because in one case out of ten feelings proved destructive; for in the general course of things, it is often feeling alone which has the power to rescue. Would I shed my blood on the day of battle for pay . . . for money or for honor? God forbid; it is too precious for that! Of course I wouldn't. But, as a free and independent man, I can nevertheless take quiet pleasure in your magnificence and majesty and in the fame and growth of your great name. That is the reward for which I sell my heart. Therefore, let's admit you break the staff above the Prince's head because of his unauthorized victory. And let's say, further, that I should one day be wandering through the woods and cliffs like a shepherd with my squadrons and there be offered a chance to bring you yet another unauthorized victory: by God, I'd be a scoundrel if I did not cheerfully repeat the Prince's act. And if you, carrying your law books in your hand, then came to me and said: "Kottwitz, you have forfeited your head," I would say: "I knew that, Your Majesty. Take it, here it is." After all, when I took an oath and bound myself, both body and soul, to your crown, I did not exempt my head. And thus I would be giving you only what was yours already.

ELECTOR: You wonderful old man, I really can't outargue you. The words you've chosen with the artful skill of an orator do sway me, I who am in any case inclined to favor you. So, I shall call an advocate to end this debate once and for all, someone who will come to my defense.

[*He rings. A servant enters.*]

ELECTOR: The Prince of Homburg . . . have him brought here from the prison!

[*The servant leaves.*]

He will teach you, I am certain, what military discipline and obedience are. At least, he's sent me a letter which puts forth quite different views than the subtle disquisitions on freedom which you've displayed here like a schoolboy. [*He crosses over to the table and reads the letter again.*]

KOTTWITZ [*astonished*]: Whom is he getting? Whom did he send for?

HENNINGS: The Prince himself?

TRUCHSS: No, it's impossible!

[*The officers gather nervously together and confer.*]

ELECTOR: And from whom is this second letter here?

HOHENZOLLERN: From me, my Lord.

ELECTOR [*reading*]: "Proof that the Elector Friedrich himself is to blame for the Prince's act" . . . now, that, by God, I call impertinent! Do you mean to say that you are trying to shove onto my shoulders responsibility for the outrage the Prince allowed himself in battle?

HOHENZOLLERN: Yes, Your Majesty, onto your shoulders! Yes, I am doing this, I, Hohenzollern.

ELECTOR: Well, this outdoes a fairy tale. One of them tries to prove the Prince is guiltless, the other that the guilty one is I myself! And how are you going to prove such an assertion?

HOHENZOLLERN: You will recall that night, Sire, when we found the Prince lying fast asleep underneath the plane trees in the garden. He was evidently dreaming of the next day's victories and held some laurel in his hands. You, in order to plumb the depths of his heart, took the wreath away from him and, with a smile, wound the chain which hangs about your neck around the wreath and handed it to Princess Natalia, your noble niece. Blushing at so wondrous a vision the Prince got up, for he wanted to seize hold of these precious things which were being offered to him by so dear a hand. You, however, leading the Princess backward, quickly moved away from him. The castle door slammed shut behind you, and . . . gone were the young lady, chain, and wreath. The Prince was left alone, standing in the well of night and carrying in his hand a glove he'd snatched from whom . . . he himself did not know.

ELECTOR: What glove is that?

HOHENZOLLERN: Let me finish the story. The whole thing was a joke to us. However, what it meant to him I was soon to learn. First I tiptoed back through the rear back gate of the garden pretending to find him there by chance. When I awoke him, he pulled himself together but a memory seemed to fill him with great joy; you cannot imagine anything more touching. Down to the smallest detail he recounted to me the whole event as if it were a dream. He said, in fact, that he'd never dreamed so vividly, and a firm conviction began to take hold of him that heaven itself had given him a sign. He believed, you see, that God would grant him on the day of the next battle everything which his vision had conjured up for him: the noble lady, the laurel wreath, and your chain of honor too!

ELECTOR: Hm! Very strange indeed! And that glove?

HOHENZOLLERN: Yes . . . this fragment of the dream that had become reality in his hand both destroyed and confirmed his belief at once. At first he looked at it in wide-eyed wonder, since it was white and from its style and form appeared to be a lady's glove. But he did not speak to any lady in the garden that night from whom he could have taken it. And because I arrived just then to call him to a meeting, his thoughts became confused and, simply forgetting what he could not comprehend, he absent-mindedly tucked the glove into his collar.

ELECTOR: Well, and then what?

HOHENZOLLERN: Then with pen and notebook in hand he entered the castle to devote his full attention to the Field Marshal's orders. But the Electress and Princess Natalia, who were about to take their leave, were also present in the room. Who could measure the great surprise that overwhelmed the Prince when the Princess noticed that she was missing the very glove that he had tucked into his collar. The Field Marshal called the Prince of Homburg's name repeatedly, to which the Prince replied: "What are my Field Marshal's orders?" He tried to collect his thoughts. But completely surrounded as he was by miracles . . . heaven's thunder could have sounded . . . [*He stops.*]

ELECTOR: Was it the Princess's glove?

HOHENZOLLERN: Of course.

[*The Elector sinks into deep thought.*]

HOHENZOLLERN [*continuing*]: Pen in hand, he stood there like a statue and merely seemed to be a living man. All his senses, however, were extinguished as if they'd been dealt a magical blow. And it was only the next morning when shots were already thundering in the ranks that he returned to life again and asked me: "What, dear friend, did Dörfling say to me when he handed out my battle orders yesterday?"

FIELD MARSHAL: My Lord, I am able to confirm this story. I recall that the Prince didn't seem to hear a word I spoke. I have often seen him in an abstracted state, but never so much as on that day.

ELECTOR: And so, if I understand you correctly, the following conclusion must tower up before me: If I had not toyed in such a dubious manner with this young dreamer's mind, he would be quite guiltless now. He would not have been distracted when he received his battle orders and would not have been obstinate in the battle. Isn't that what you're driving at? Is that not so?

HOHENZOLLERN: My Lord, you may draw your own conclusion.

ELECTOR: Fool that you are, you idiot! Had you not called me down into the garden, I would not have given in to curiosity and would therefore not have played my harmless little joke upon the dreamer. Therefore, I assert with equal right that the person with whom blame should lie for the Prince's error . . . is not me, but you yourself! Oh, what Delphic wisdom my officers possess!

HOHENZOLLERN: I have said enough, my Lord. I'm certain my words won't fail to have an effect.

SCENE 6

[*An officer enters. The above.*]

OFFICER: The Prince will be here shortly, Your Majesty.

ELECTOR: Good. Have him come in.

OFFICER: It'll be a few minutes yet. As he was on his way here, he stopped to ask a watchman to open the churchyard gate.

ELECTOR: The churchyard gate?

OFFICER: Yes, my sovereign Lord.

ELECTOR: For what purpose?

OFFICER: To tell the truth, I do not know. It seems he wished to see the grave to which your orders have condemned him.

[*The officers gather together and confer.*]

ELECTOR: It doesn't matter. Have him come in as soon as he arrives. [*He steps up to the table once again and examines his papers.*]

TRUCHSS: Here come the guards now escorting the Prince.

SCENE 7

[*The Prince of Homburg enters. An officer with the guards. The above.*]

ELECTOR: My young Prince, I call on you for help. Colonel Kottwitz has brought me this petition on your behalf. Please look at it; it's been signed by a hundred noblemen and says the army demands your freedom and cannot accept the verdict of the military court. Read and judge it for yourself, I beg you! [*He gives him the document.*]

PRINCE [*After studying the paper briefly, he turns and looks at the circle of officers standing by.*] Kottwitz, old friend, let me shake your hand. You've done more for me today than I earned from you on the day of battle. But now hurry back to Arnstein from where you came and do not budge from there. I have considered the matter and wish to die according to the sentence. [*He hands the petition back to Kottwitz.*]

KOTTWITZ [*taken aback*]: No, my Prince, that can't be. What are you saying?

HOHENZOLLERN: He wants to die?

TRUCHSS: He should not . . . must not die!

SEVERAL OFFICERS [*pressing forward*]: My Lord and Sovereign! Your Majesty! Hear us!

PRINCE: Be silent! It is my inflexible will! I want to glorify the sacred laws of war which I have broken in full view of the army. I want to die a freely chosen death. How important can a small victory be for you, my brothers, which I perhaps might win from Wrangel? How can you compare this with my glorious triumph tomorrow morning over the most destructive enemies which we harbor in ourselves: defiance and arrogance! Let the foreigner who tries to subjugate us fall and may the people of Brandenburg assert their freedom on our maternal ground. For this earth is theirs and its meadows' splendor belongs to them alone.

KOTTWITZ [*moved*]: My son! My dearest friend! What can I call you now?

TRUCHSS: Oh, God of the world.

KOTTWITZ: Let me kiss your hand!

[*They press around him.*]

PRINCE [*to the Elector*]: With great emotion, I submit to you, my Lord, whom I was once privileged to call by a dearer name, a privilege I have frivolously thrown away. Forgive me if I served you too impetuously on that fateful day: death now washes me clean of all my guilt. Reconciled and cheerful, I freely accede to the verdict of your laws. So comfort me in turn with the knowledge that you no longer bear a grudge against me. And in this hour of farewell, grant me a sign of your grace to confirm that I'm forgiven.

ELECTOR: Speak, young hero. What is it you wish? I pledge my word and my honor as a knight that whatever your wish may be, it shall be granted.

PRINCE: Your Majesty, do not buy peace from Gustave Karl with the hand of your niece. Expel from the camp the Swedish go-between whose proposals rob you of your honor. Answer him with cannon shot instead.

ELECTOR [*kissing him on the forehead*]: It shall be as you have asked. With this kiss, my son, I grant you your last wish. Why should there yet be one more sacrifice which was, in any case, torn from me only by the vicissitudes of war? From now on, every word you've spoken will flower into a victory which will crush the Swedish enemy. I'll write King Gustave that Princess Natalia is Prince Friedrich of Homburg's bride . . . the Prince who fell according to the law for the sake of Fehrbellin. Let the Swedish king fight for her on the field of battle where the Prince's spirit will still march in the vanguard with the flags of Brandenburg, though he lies dead. [*He kisses him once again and raises him.*]

PRINCE: Now you've given me my life again. And now I'll pray for every blessing from above, for every glory that the Seraphim enthroned in clouds pour down so joyously upon the heads of heroes. Go and wage war, oh Lord, and conquer the entire world if it defies you. For you deserve such victory.

ELECTOR: Guards! Take him back to prison.

SCENE 8

[*Natalia and the Electress appear at the door, followed by ladies-in-waiting. The above.*]

NATALIA: Oh, mother! Why do you speak to me of what is proper? The most seemly act at such an hour is to love him . . . my dearest, most unfortunate friend!

PRINCE [*leaving*]: Take me away!

TRUCHSS [*restraining him*]: No, my Prince, you can't do this.

[*Several officers block the way.*]

PRINCE: Take me away!

HOHENZOLLERN: My Elector, can your heart . . . ?

PRINCE [*tearing himself free*]: You tyrants! Do you want me to be dragged in chains to the place of execution? Go away! I have closed my accounts with life. [*He leaves with the guards.*]

NATALIA [*laying her head upon her aunt's shoulder*]: Oh, earth, take me to your bosom too! Why should I gaze at the sunlight any longer?

SCENE 9

[*The above without the Prince of Homburg.*]

FIELD MARSHAL: Oh, God of the world! Did it have to come to this?

[*The Elector speaks secretly and urgently with an officer.*]

KOTTWITZ [*in a cold voice*]: My sovereign Lord and Master, are we now dismissed after all that's passed?

ELECTOR: No! Not yet. I'll let you know when you're dismissed. [*He stares at him for a short while. Then he takes the papers which the page has brought from the table and turns to the Field Marshal.*] Give this pass to the Swedish Count Horn. It is my cousin, the Prince's last will which I am obliged to fulfill. The cease-fire will end in three days, and battle will commence. [*Pause. He casts a look at the death warrant.*] Well, judge for yourself, gentlemen. In the past year alone, the Prince of Homburg with his defiance and frivolity has cost me two of my most precious victories. At Fehrbellin he seriously interfered yet with a third one. Now that he's passed through the schooling of these last few days, would you be prepared to risk a fourth with him?

KOTTWITZ AND TRUCHSS [*together*]: What, my godlike, my divine . . . ?

ELECTOR: Are you willing? Do you dare?

KOTTWITZ: By heaven, you could be standing at the edge of doom and the Prince wouldn't lift a finger to help you; he wouldn't save your life unless you gave the order.

ELECTOR [*tearing up the death warrant*]: Well, friends, so come and follow me into the garden now.

[*They all leave.*]

SCENE 10

Scene: The castle, with a ramp leading down into the garden as in Act One.

[*It is night again. The Prince of Homburg is being led blind-folded by Cavalry Captain Strantz through the lower garden gate. The Prince's guard with its officers are present. In the distance, drums beating a funeral march are heard.*]

PRINCE: Now, immortality, you are totally mine! You are streaming toward me with the radiance of a thousand suns through the blindfold on my eyes. Wings are growing on my shoulders, and my spirit is already soaring through the calm ethereal spheres. And like a ship which, borne away by winds, sees the cheerful harbor disappear, so all of life is sinking away from me in twilight. I can still perceive colors and shapes, but everything beneath me is lying in a mist.

[*The Prince sits down on a bench which has been set up underneath an oak tree in the middle of the garden. Cavalry Captain Strantz moves away from him and looks up toward the ramp.*]

PRINCE: Oh, how wonderfully fragrant the violets are! Don't you smell them?

[*Strantz returns to him.*]

STRANTZ: They are carnations and garden pinks.

PRINCE: Garden pinks? How do they come to be growing here?

STRANTZ: I don't know. It seems a young girl has planted them here. May I give you a carnation?

PRINCE: Thank you, friend. I will put it in water when I get home.

SCENE 11

[*The Elector enters holding a laurel wreath about which is wound his golden chain. He is followed by the Electress,*

Princess Natalia, Field Marshal Dörfling, Colonel Kottwitz, Hohenzollern, Goltz, and so forth. Ladies-in-waiting, officers, and pages with torches appear on the ramp. Hohenzollern, carrying a scarf, appears at the balustrade and signals to Cavalry Captain Strantz, who then withdraws from the Prince and speaks in the background with the guards.]

PRINCE: Friend, what is this radiance that's spreading its light around me?

STRANTZ [*returning to him*]: My Prince, will you kindly rise?

PRINCE: What's happening?

STRANTZ: Nothing that should cause you fear. I merely wish to untie the blindfold on your eyes.

PRINCE: Has the last hour of my suffering come?

STRANTZ: Yes! Hail to you and accept all our blessings, for you are worthy of them.

[*The Elector gives the wreath on which the necklace hangs to the Princess, takes her by the hand, and escorts her down the ramp. Ladies and gentlemen follow. The Princess, surrounded by torches, steps in front of the Prince who looks up in amazement. She places the wreath on his head, hangs the chain around his neck, and presses his hand to her heart. The Prince faints.*]

NATALIA: Joy is killing him!

HOHENZOLLERN [*catching him*]: Help!

ELECTOR: Let the thunder of the cannon rouse him!

[*Cannon shot. A March. The castle is illuminated.*]

KOTTWITZ: Hail, hail to the Prince of Homburg!

OFFICER: Hail! Hail! Hail!

ALL: To the victor of the battle of Fehrbellin!

91

[*A moment of silence.*]

PRINCE: No, tell me, is it a dream?

KOTTWITZ: A dream, what else?

SEVERAL OFFICERS: Into the field of battle! Into the field!

TRUCHSS: To the battle!

FIELD MARSHAL: On to victory! On to victory!

ALL: Into the dust with all the enemies of Brandenburg.

CURTAIN